5⁵⁰

New eyes for reading

New eyes for reading

Biblical and theological reflections by women from the third world

EDITED BY JOHN S. POBEE AND
BÄRBEL VON WARTENBERG-POTTER

MEYER
STONE
BOOKS

First published in 1986 by World Council of Churches, 50 route de Ferney, 1211 Geneva 20, Switzerland

First U.S. edition published in 1987 by Meyer•Stone Books, 2014 South Yost Avenue, Bloomington, IN 47403

Typeset in Switzerland and printed and bound in the United States of America

Meyer•Stone ISBN 0-940-989-07-7

Contents

Preface

New eyes for reading — yes, indeed, in all ages we need to make a fresh approach to our ancient texts and traditions in order to rediscover their importance and relevance for our lives.

Here are some of the discoveries that women make today as they see and read their own tradition with a sharpened consciousness.

They challenge us in at least three ways.

1. They clearly indicate the context from which the women write. They are third world women, discovering for themselves the social, religious, political and economic realities amidst which they live. They reflect on God's word from within their situations, however different these may be from one third world country to another.

2. They express the theological and spiritual discoveries which women have made. This may be considered to be a limitation, but no claim whatever is made for universal validity nor do they seek to impose insights on others as traditional Western theology has sometimes done. It is one of the basic requirements of every honest theology to recognize its own limitations and biases. Only through such admission can an authentic ecumenical dialogue be initiated. This hermeneutical premise calls our attention to the fact that for too long theology was a field — cornered first by learned Western men of the North, then by the learned men of the North and the South — where only in recent times women have been able to make their voices heard, whether in the North or the South. The absence of women's voices in the field of theological thinking and spiritual leadership has impoverished the churches. These reflections represent a humble effort to bridge this gap. They also illustrate the fact that women's theology and feminist approaches to the Bible and Tradition are not the prerogative of Western women.

3. The pieces included here represent reflections on biblical texts and reflections on the situation of women in the churches. They are part of an

ongoing dialogue between women in the ecumenical movement about their responsibility to further the ecumenical debate and to renew their own churches. There can be no renewal of the churches if the new roles of women and their participation are ignored. But women who raise critical questions are often in a minority, and we need a global dialogue and a global sisterhood to strengthen one another in the local situation, to help one another to grow in understanding of and become sensitive to the diversity of situations in which women do theology today. In many churches the number of women theological students is growing rapidly. Women assume leadership positions in greater numbers.

The World Council of Churches' Sub-unit on Women in Church and Society has been deeply committed to encourage women's theology. We are happy to present this collection in cooperation with the Sub-unit on Theological Education; it too has a commitment to the contribution of women in the theological field.

John Pobee   Bärbel von Wartenberg-Potter

Part I

New Eyes
for Reading

I. The Woman Who Decided to Break the Rules

Elizabeth Amoah

> And there was a woman who had had a flow of blood for twelve years, and who had suffered much under many physicians, and had spent all that she had, and was not better but rather grew worse. She had heard the reports about Jesus, and came up behind him in the crowd and touched his garment. For she said: 'If I touch even his garments, I shall be made well.' And immediately the hemorrhage ceased; and she felt in her body that she was healed of her disease (Mark 5:25-29).

Naturally the weak, pale woman in this story was poor and frustrated. Added to her physical misery were the requirements of the Israelite ceremonial laws about impurities, as stipulated in Leviticus 15:19ff.

The plight of this woman would have been even worse had she lived in my country. Among the Akan of Ghana, women used to be considered abnormal during their menstrual period.

The custom was that, during the days of her period, a woman not only had to observe numerous restrictions — she was not allowed to cross the threshold of any man's house, nor was she allowed to perform the regular duties of a wife like cooking the meals — but she even had to leave her own home and live alone in the *bra dan*, the "house for menstruation" on the outskirts of the village.

Hence, one of the euphemisms which the Akan used to describe a woman in her menstrual period was "she has gone to the outskirts of town", *w'ako mfikyire*.

The blood of such women was considered potent enough to neutralize or defeat evil powers. Parallel ideas are found in many other cultures.

Because of her disease, the unnamed woman with the hemorrhage whom Mark portrays must have suffered from financial problems. She also faced social, cultural and religious difficulties. She had to move carefully, in order not to make someone else unclean by coming into contact with him or her.

The unnamed woman in this account had been living in that kind of frustrating isolation for twelve years. She had no hope of being healed — until Jesus came.

On the basis of the rules and regulations set forth in Leviticus 15, the woman must be very much aware that she ought not to go out and mingle with the crowd following Jesus.

Yet — whether out of superstition or out of a more genuine sort of trust and faith in Jesus — she is stubbornly convinced that if only she can touch even Jesus' garment all her years of frustration will be over.

Like any other person who has been hemmed in for years by traditions and customs, she debates with herself. Shoud she try to touch Jesus and perhaps be healed? Or should she abide by the religious rules and live with her disease and frustration?

Whatever any of us might suppose to be the appropriate decision in similar circumstances, there is a proverb in Akan that is very much to the point: "It is the person who is very near the fire who feels how hot the fire is" *(nya oben gya no na onyim ma ogya no hyehye fa)*.

This woman has been very near the fire. She knows what she has been going through for twelve long years. She knows how desperately she needs to be cured.

And so she decides to break the rules. She touches Jesus. That challenging and daring action results not only in her immediate healing but also in words of commendation from Jesus: "Daughter, your faith has made you well; go in peace, and be healed of your disease" (Mark 5:34).

In one sense, the story of the encounter between the unnamed woman with a hemorrhage and Jesus is a woman's story. The presence of Jesus, it tells us, enables us to challenge and question all sorts of customs and traditions that enslave us and make us frustrated.

But the experience of this woman and the lessons this story teaches us represent a challenge to all Christians. They apply to all kinds of situations in human life.

True salvation always challenges existing laws and regulations. But it calls for awareness and effort on the part of the person who seeks salvation.

II. The Woman Who Complicated the History of Salvation

Elsa Tamez

Introduction

All Christians, and especially Christians immersed in the process of liberation, believe that the Bible has a liberating message for life. God is seen as liberator through God's works on behalf of the oppressed (for example, with Israel when it was oppressed, and later with the poor people of Israel). The fundamental event, according to Severino Croatto, Argentinian biblical scholar, is the Exodus, which generates new facts with each study. One celebrates liberation not as a simple act of triumphant grace, but also as recognition of faith in a liberator God, who still is liberating. Belief in God arises from the experience of liberation in the Exodus, and in other critical stages. This guideline is reinterpreted in the Bible in new situations and with new meanings.

I believe that another great guideline paralleling the Exodus is the teaching of Jesus Christ, which is a rereading of the same Exodus. It enables us to read the whole biblical text from a perspective of liberation.

There are in the Bible re-workings of events originally grounded in particular meanings, events actualizing faith in situations of crisis reworked because their original impact had faded. They are re-read not with the intellectual curiosity to understand the past, but with the need to respond to life situations today. Our present, according to Carlos Mesters, enters and functions as filter, criterion, and light in the search for meaning in biblical texts.

Even though the cataloguing of the books of the Bible is complete, the presence of God goes on. Christian women, motivated by the Spirit, search their daily life for this liberation God of the Exodus, and for Jesus

---

● This article has been translated into English by Betsy Yeager. It was published in the original Spanish in *Media Development*, journal of the World Association for Christian Communication, Vol. XXXI, No. 2, May 1984.

Christ who carries on God's work today. Women, who are oriented by this kind of thinking, will never take as a norm any text that seems to sanction their submission.

Bible study from this perspective is full of conflict. Women hear the voice of God favouring them. Most men don't hear this because they come from a tradition that believes that they are chosen because of their masculinity. This conflict is healthy. It makes us think about what conversion really is, of the New Person in every facet of understanding. This includes radically changing the masculine, or macho, attitude in theoretical terms, in practice and through personal conviction.

But beware! To read the Bible from the perspective of a third world woman involves putting two women in a situation of conflict. This we shall do in our present re-reading.

An oppressed woman: Hagar

Generally, when church people speak of women in the Bible they choose to highlight famous women like Deborah, Esther the queen, Sarah, Mary. They never mention women slaves who were pagan, or poor, such as Hagar, the slave Sarah brought from Egypt. Hagar will be for traditional Bible study a negative model, because she became rebellious and wouldn't submit to Sarah's wishes.

On reading the stories of Sarah and Hagar (Gen. 16:1-4; 21:8-20) we generally identify ourselves with Sarah, the beautiful wife of the great patriarch Abraham, the father of the faith. We do this for two reasons. First, because the stories are so constructed as to lead the reader to such identification, and because Sarah's role is crucial in the history of Israel. Second, because the story continually emphasizes the submission of the workers, and the attitude of Sarah towards Hagar appears quite natural.

Right at the beginning we must recognize these two elements, and consciously distance ourselves from them, in order to read the text, or perhaps reconstruct it, from the perspective of third world women.

This incident, which does not appear strange to domestic workers today, happened thousands of years ago, during the third dynasty of Ur, and the twelfth Egyptian dynasty. It comes to us from two sources: Yahwistic, Gen. 16,[1] written down in the tenth century B.C., and the Elohistic, Gen. 21,[2] of the eighth century B.C. Both chapters are perhaps

---

[1] Verses 1, 3 and 15 are sacerdotal.

[2] Verses 1 and 2 are a mixture of Yahweh and Elohim; verses 3 to 5 are sacerdotal.

variants of the same story,[3] or perhaps deal with two separate situations.[4] This does not concern us in this particular study because, although there are certain differences, especially in the actions and personalities of the characters, we are going to read the story as it appears in the biblical text, and will take the 21st chapter as a continuation of the 16th. Neither will we take into account the possible etiologies in the texts (the existence of the Ishmaelites, and the Lahai Roi well), for following Von Rad, we believe that the central issues do not come from etiologies.[5] Our intention is to read the story as it is actually recorded, from the perspective of the slave woman.

Hagar and Ishmael complicate the history of salvation

Everything was well-planned for Abraham and Sarah, but a woman and her son broke into the story, complicating it. Who is Hagar?

Hagar is a slave in the service of Sarah. There were few slaves at that time, and most of them were in domestic service. Only fairly wealthy people kept slaves.[6] Abraham and Sarah were a wealthy couple, and considered their wealth as a gift from God, a common Hebrew attitude. Slaves were treated as property; they were bought and sold. Their value was between 20 and 40 shekels. There were distinct classes of slaves — prisoners of war who had been reduced to slaves, some who had been bought, children of slaves who were raised in the owners' homes, some who sold themselves into slavery because of poverty.[7] There were various laws in the Torah which were meant to make the lives of these slaves more tolerable, from which we must deduce that they were oppressed.

Relations between Egypt and Asia were peaceful[8] at that time. Therefore Hagar could not have been a prisoner of war sold to Abraham. Probably Hagar was sold to Sarah as her servant. She could have been an "apiru"[9] who had sold herself into slavery because of her extreme

---

[3] Skinner, *International Critical Commentary, Genesis*, London, Edinburgh, 1980, p.285.

[4] Gerhard Von Rad, *El Libro del Génesis*, Salamanca, Sígueme, 1977, p.239.

[5] *Ibid.*, although we disagree with him when he stresses that the insertion of the statement is due to the fact that the editor intends to delay the fulfilment of the promise.

[6] J. A. Larraya, "Esclavo", *Enciclopedia de la Biblia*, Barcelona, Ed. Garriga SA, 1964, Vol. III, p.100.

[7] *Ibid.*, pp.100-104.

[8] E. Cassin *et al.*, *Los Imperios del Antiguo Oriente*, Mexico, Siglo XXI, 1974, p.287.

[9] A difficult term to define, it appears in Ugaratic, Acadic, Egyptian and other ancient languages, and it was applied to a group of people who were marginal, mercenary, bandits, thieves, poor, landless, subversive, without ethnic identity, etc.

poverty. The text does not explain how Hagar came to be Sarah's slave, but it says explicitly that she was indeed Sarah's slave.[10] Hagar was the type of slave who looked after her mistress, did domestic work, and served as wet nurse for the children of her mistress.

Hagar was Egyptian, a point distinctly against her. Strangers in Israel were discriminated against, and were counted among the least important — widows, orphans, and the poor. They were oppressed. Hebrew law repeatedly prohibits the abuse of servants. Hebrew solidarity extended only to the Hebrew race. For this reason they took foreigners as slaves; they did not want to subject fellow Israelites to such treatment. Foreign slaves remained slaves in perpetuity, whereas Hebrew slaves could recover their liberty in the Jubilee Year. Hagar was destined to serve Sarah till she died, unless her owners should decide to give her her liberty.

Because Hagar is a woman she is a person oppressed three times over, owing to her slave status, her race, and her sex. As we know, Israel was a patriarchal society, and women definitely occupied a low second place in it.

So here we have this Egyptian woman who upsets God's magnificent plans for Sarah and Abraham.

God promised descendants to Abraham, but his wife could bear no children. It has been said that this is to show that with God nothing is impossible. That is the Yahwistic interpretation, of interest to the reader. But why not say that this happens to reveal to the oppressed peoples of the earth the story of salvation?

The barrenness that Sarah suffered was even more terrible as she came from the Eastern world. But her sterility is a blessing for Hagar, for she will carry the first-born of Abraham.

Sarah refuses to accept her own sterility. She must provide descendants for Abraham, and she resorts to the laws of the families of the Hurrites with which she was very familiar. Sarah gave Abraham her slave as a concubine. It was quite common in the Mediterranean region for wives to give their slaves as concubines to their husbands, that they might have descendants. Rachel and Leah do so. In these cases the children of the slaves are the legitimate children of the owner.

Hagar became pregnant. This is the first appearance of Hagar in the story (chap. 15). God promised Abraham a line of descendants, and in the

---

[10] In chapter 16 the Hebrew word *shafjat* is used, and in 21 *a'mah*; these are synonymous for a maid or slave.

very next chapter Hagar is pregnant by Abraham. The promise is completed here, for a son will be born to Abraham (Gen. 15:4). It would be quite acceptable according to the family codes of that time. It wasn't exactly ideal for Abraham and his lineage, nor for the Hebrew culture. The foreign blood, that of a slave in particular, would obscure the lineage.

The beautiful Hebrew woman was eventually able to bear her husband a child (chap. 18) in order that the promise of descendants would be accomplished without presenting problems to the narrator, the culture and the tradition. But there was Ishmael, the son of the slave Hagar, who cannot be erased from history and will always be demanding his rights as the first-born and legitimate son of Abraham.

The appearance of Hagar and Ishmael in the patriarchal history is not a simple trick to add suspense or interest to the story. It may appear so from a literary point of view, but that is not its true significance. If this story was gathered through traditions and included in biblical history, it is because it has a lesson for us. The marginalized demand as first-born sons to be included in the history of salvation. They break the order of things. They complicate history.

Hagar rejects her slavery

On changing from the position of servant to that of concubine, and awaiting the child of Abraham, Hagar suddenly realizes what her slavery means. God will bless her with a son, and she is not going to renounce her right to him and give him to her mistress. Furthermore, she breaks with legal tradition, believing herself a person equal in status to her former mistress. She no longer feels herself a slave without the right to make decisions. She is the pregnant wife of her master, involved with him in the completion of God's promise. Perhaps Hagar realized that she was a stranger and a slave, but she also knew that Amenemes I was not of royal blood, as the prophet Nepherty[11] had announced, and had nevertheless founded the 12th dynasty in Egypt. Possibly she thought Abraham was on her side, and wouldn't pay any attention to the laws. However Sarah demanded that they be followed. In verse 5 Sarah cites a judicial formula to help her seek legal protection:[12] "My offence falls on your shoulders; I let my slave sleep with you, but you look at me with distaste now that you see her pregnant…"

---

[11] Cassin, *op. cit.*, p.272.
[12] Von Rad, *op. cit.* p.235.1

The Hammurabi Code imposed a penalty on slaves who, on becoming concubines, try to gain equal status with the legal wife. The first part of this does not fit Sarah, but the second does:

> A priestess of the rank of Naditum who is free to marry, but not to have children, gives a slave to her husband to have children by. If this concubine tries to create a sense of equality between herself and the legal wife, the wife has the right to send her back to slavery, but not to sell her to others (Cod. Ham. 146).

Sarah saw her rights as wife and mistress threatened. She preferred to maintain her position as wife above that of giving Abraham a son, who of course was his according to tradition.[13]

Abraham chose to obey Sarah, and the law, against the feelings of Hagar or the interests of the son. Hagar loses. Abraham breaks relations with Hagar and gives her back to Sarah. Hagar is demoted to her old status of slave. However Sarah wasn't pleased with this. She couldn't send Hagar away because of the law (Cod. Ham. 146) which prohibited it in these circumstances, but she ill-treated her (v.6) — to such an extent that Hagar fled in spite of all the dangers of the desert.

If Sarah oppressed her more than ever, it was perhaps because Hagar resisted her. She did not want Hagar to return to her old legal status. She had rejected her slavery. She was not interested in trying to win Sarah's goodwill by suffering the abuses in silence. Hagar preferred to die in the desert. There were only two alternatives left to Hagar: subject herself to the humiliations inflicted on her or die in the desert. She chose the second.[14]

Hagar and Ishmael, marginalized in history (Gen. 21)

It is a scenario familiar to domestic servants today. The servant is thrown out of the house because she bears a son to the master of the house, because she is powerless to resist him. She is taken as an object, and thrown out as an object.

There is a great celebration. Sarah is content because her own child, Isaac, has been weaned. He is three years old, at which time it is customary to wean children. Everyone is happy because the second child

---

[13] Luis Alonso Schökel and Juan Mateos, *Pentateuco I, Génesis y Exodo*, Madrid, Ed. Cristiandad, 1970, p.74.

[14] In this chapter Hagar does not come back, and gives birth in the desert. Verse 9 is a later addition, made in order to give continuity to the narrative in chapter 21. Cf. Von Rad, Skinner, Schökel, Speiser (*Génesis*, New York, Doubleday, Anchor Bible, 1982) and others.

of the master has come through the risks of infant death, and entered a new stage of development. The little brothers Ishmael and Isaac play together in the innocence of childhood.

This picture of the children makes us remember that Sarah no longer needs Ishmael, her adopted son. Her own son, Isaac, has now passed safely through the dangers of early childhood. Ishmael, the son of Abraham but not of Sarah, ought to leave so that he will have no share of the inheritance.

The attitude of Sarah is egotistical and cruel, and we must recognize this. Some commentaries have tried to soften it. They say that Ishmael didn't play with Isaac, but that he made fun[15] of him, and this upset his mother, Sarah. However, according to Speiser: "There is nothing in the text to suggest that Ishmael was abusing Isaac; it's a theme deduced by readers trying to soften the actions of Sarah."[16]

The text presents us with the problem of Ishmael's age. Obviously the narrator (Elohistic) makes him a little older than Isaac, for Abraham, when he says goodbye to him, places him on the shoulders of Hagar (v.14) and later in the desert she lays him beneath a bush (v.15). However, according to priestly sources the boy must have been 17 years old.

This also has been used as an excuse for Sarah's cruelty. If Ishmael really is 17 years old, and continues to bother and make fun of little Isaac, the mother is bound to react to protect her child. But our Elohistic narrator paints such a sweet picture of the two playing together during the celebration that we must conclude that Sarah acted the way she did because she wanted to be the only wife in the house, and mother of the promised descendant and inheritor, and not because she had more vision than Abraham, or followed God's plans any better, as has been frequently stated. God let her act that way because he had other plans for Hagar, a better future than in the house of Abraham.

In this chapter, Hagar isn't the servant of Sarah, but only a slave of the house who happened to be the master's concubine; however Sarah begs Abraham, the head of the household, to throw her out, and her son too: "And she said to Abraham: 'Say goodbye to that servant, for that

---

[15] The Hebrew word *msajak* means "to play", "to laugh"; if it is to mean to ridicule, to mock someone, it should be preceded by a *b*.Cf. Skinner, *op. cit.*, p.322.

[16] Speiser, *op. cit.*, p.155.

servant's son is not going to inherit equally with my child, Isaac'" (Gen. 21:10).

Sarah is not referring to Ishmael as Abraham's son, she only sees the blood of the Egyptian slave in him; furthermore in this chapter she never refers to Hagar, but rather to "that servant", a disrespectful phrase. Sarah, then, is pointing out the social inequalities. Ishmael is different from Isaac for he is the child of "that servant", while Isaac is the son of the proper wife in the home.

Sarah's petition to Abraham goes against the existing laws of that time. Sarah breaks with legality because it doesn't serve her purposes. The child born of a slave cannot be thrown out of the house. The ruling law in that region recognized the right of election of the child of the legal wife, but not of inheritance. Furthermore, the adopted child of the slave, in this case Ishmael, was equal to Isaac insofar as inheritance was concerned (Cod. Ham. 170). "No one can change that legislation, not even the mistress of the house, and by that very law she could never throw the child of Hagar out."[17] Sarah resorted to the law when it served her purposes, and broke it when that was more convenient for her.

Abraham at first rejected her appeal. He loved his child deeply, and perhaps also Hagar, a fact which, in passing, might also be another reason Sarah appears so jealous.[18] Also, perhaps Abraham didn't want to break the law.

Abraham bid them goodbye with a heavy heart, by decree of the angel of the Lord (we will meet him later), and not because of Sarah. The narrator presents a scene heavy with sadness:

> Getting up at dawn, Abraham gave bread and a wineskin of water to Hagar, put the child on her shoulders, and turned them out (v.14).

Hagar was not the rebellious, haughty person that we read about in chapter 16. Here it is painful to see her headed in the direction of the desert with her son. In this chapter she is not fleeing by her own decision, she is merely doing what Sarah and Abraham decreed. Hagar is not rebelling against this injustice, but neither is she begging them not to throw her out. She leaves to enjoy a greater liberty: she is Ishmael's sole parent now; neither Abraham nor Sarah can claim any rights over him. She will have to struggle very hard, for she must be both mother and father to him.

Sarah's intention is to erase them from history, and make herself the only mother of the promised people, but what of the blood of Abraham in

---

[17] Emanuelle Testa, *Genesi*, Rome, Ed. Pauline, 1972, p.210.
[18] Schökel and Mateos, *op. cit.*, p.75.

Ishmael? Who can erase that? Only if they die in the desert will that threat be eliminated.

God blesses Hagar and Ishmael

Twice Hagar stopped in the desert, and both times the angel of the Lord saved her.[19] The first time he found her pregnant, near a spring (16:7), the second time on the point of dying from thirst (21:16). Each time God saved her and blessed her.

In her first encounter with God Hagar almost didn't believe that she had seen God; in the second she didn't doubt it, for God had saved her and her baby, when they were on the verge of death.

Hagar the slave is the only woman in the Old Testament who had the experience of a theophany (chap. 16). This is most important. The great men of the Bible like Abraham, Moses and Jacob, founders of the Hebrew faith, had experienced visions of God, but Hagar is an Egyptian slave woman. How could she have the privilege of seeing and talking with God? Could it be simply that God felt compassion for her there in the desert? Hagar experienced this manifestation because God wished to point out that the oppressed are also God's children, co-creators of history. God does not leave them to perish in the desert without leaving a trace. They must live to be part of history, and struggle to be subjects of it.

In chapter 16, before Ishmael was born, Hagar was surprised that God should be interested in her, a housemaid, a pagan, a woman. She says: "Can it be that I have come to see the one who sees me?" (Jerusalem Bible). Perhaps it had never occurred to Hagar that God might come near to her, for she was a slave. Therefore she wasn't certain that what was happening to her could be real. Perhaps she asked herself: Truly does he see me, care for me? Can I be interesting to him? I'm not one of the tribe of Abraham.

Strangely enough Hagar gives God a name, the God who sees,[20] because this God saw her oppression and offered her great plans for the future of her son.

---

[19] In Hebrew *Mal'ak*, messenger. The angel of Yahweh or Elohim "personalizes the word and action of God, which God directs to earth". Westermann and Jenni, *Diccionario Teológico*, Manual del ATI, Madrid, Cristiandad, 1978, p.1232. For Von Rad, there is no difference here between the angel of the Lord and Yahweh himself, *op. cit.*, p.236.

[20] The Hebrew sentence presents a translation problem. We have followed the translation of the Jerusalem Bible.

When the angel of the Lord found her disoriented in the desert he asked her: "Hagar, slave of Sarah, where do you come from, and where are you going?" These are not simply rhetorical questions, they are full of meaning.[21] They cover her whole life. "From whence do you come" reflects her whole past. It involves related questions such as: "How have you lived your life in the house of Abraham and Sarah? What have you made of it? What do you think of your past? What have you done for yourself? What have they done for you?" "Where are you going" is future-oriented. "What are your plans? What are your hopes? your dreams? In what do you believe?"

In a valiant, honest way Hagar answers only the first question — "I'm fleeing my mistress, Sarah." With that she expresses her rejection of slavery, her past life, the ill-treatment at the hands of her mistress. Insofar as the second question is concerned Hagar is silent, she doesn't know what to say or do. She is disoriented. She didn't have time to make plans. She simply fled from oppression.

From verse 9, chapter 16 the plot perplexes us. Scholars say that this was inserted later.[22] However we cannot put it aside. We are re-reading the text in its final form, and according to canon, we must interpret these words according to the re-reading.

The angel of the Lord counsels Hagar to return and subject herself to Sarah, her old mistress from whom she has been liberated. Indeed! Counsel of the Lord! God on the side of the oppressors, she might think, and so might we. Understood in this manner, it simply doesn't go with the text. God's plans are not for Hagar to return to the oppression. According to some scholars, God wants her to return because Yahweh won't tolerate the breaking of the laws.[23] What God wants is that she and her child should be saved, and at the moment, the only way to accomplish that is not in the desert, but by returning to the house of Abraham. Ishmael hasn't been born. The first three years of life are crucial. Hagar simply must wait a little longer, because Ishmael must be born in the house of Abraham to prove that he is the first-born (Deut. 21:15-17), and to enter into the household through the rite of circumcision (chap. 17). This will guarantee him participation in the history of salvation, and will give him rights of inheritance in the house of Abraham.

---

[21] Von Rad, *op. cit.*, p.237.

[22] See note 14.

[23] This is what Von Rad thinks, *op. cit.*, p.237.

It certainly must have been difficult for Hagar to accept this proposal of God. But God had said: "I will multiply your descendants in such a fashion that you won't be able to count them" (16:10).

To ensure the realization of this promise she will have to ensure the life of her son.

God guaranteed all this to her, announcing ahead of time the baby's name, what he will be, and what he will do in history.

All this confirmed the fact that God had seen her affliction. The words of verse 11, "because Yahweh has heard your affliction", remind us of the words of God to Moses about the life of the Hebrews in Egypt: "I have heard them cry out in the presence of their oppressors; therefore I know their suffering" (Ex. 3:7). Strangely in our story the subjects are reversed. Here the Hebrews are comfortable, and it is they who are oppressing an Egyptian slave.

It is significant to note the manner in which God addresses Hagar; what we have is the classic form of "annunciation".[24] We see the elements (look, you have conceived); the birth (and you will bear a son); the name of the child (whom you will call Ishmael); the significance of the name (because Yahweh has heard your affliction); and the future of the son (he will be a wild-ass of a man, his hand against all, and the hand of all against him, and he will place his tent in front of all his brothers).

Doesn't this remind us of the annunciation? Mary also called herself a slave, a humble servant of the Lord.

The second encounter of Hagar with God occurs in chapter 21, in which Ishmael appears. This scene is sadder. There is no water, and her son is on the verge of death from thirst.

In chapter 16 God initiates the dialogue; here Hagar takes the initiative, crying out because she can't bear to see her son die. As a matter of fact she has put him far from her sight under a bush (v.15).

She cries desperately, without the slightest hope. God speaks to her from the heavens (Elohistic style), and asks her: What is the trouble, Hagar? God didn't ask her about the past, or the future, only the present. Her present is agony, anxiety and desperation. In chapter 16 Hagar, who had fled by her own decision, found a spring of water, accompanied by a theophany. Now she is in the desert, alone, with her dying child, without the possibility of returning to the tribe, because she had been thrown out, and there is no spring from which to drink. For this reason, at this moment, this hour, the present, she cries in desperation. She is not

---

[24] Schökel and Mateos, *op. cit.*, p.76.

thinking of the past or the future, only of the desperate need of the present, which could mean life for her son. — What's the trouble, Hagar?

Hagar doesn't answer, perhaps because God gave her no opportunity to speak, or perhaps because the situation said everything, and silence speaks more loudly.

God, in solidarity, comforts her: Fear not, I have heard the child from where he is. Get up! Pick up the child, and take him by the hand, because I have converted him into a great nation (v.18).

Before giving her water God gives her courage, spirit, and hope. God has heard the cry of Ishmael; he is called Ishmael, because God is, and always will be, ready to hear the cries of the son of a slave. Ishmael signifies in Hebrew "God hears", and God will always listen to children such as Ishmael who are the victims of injustice.

Hagar simply has to stop crying, in spite of everything. She has to pick herself up, pick up the child and teach him to struggle against the hardships of the desert. She has to take hold of the hand of the child forcefully, that is to say with strength, and courage.[25] This was the role of the father in Eastern traditions. In our story it is Hagar, the mother, who has to struggle alone, with a strong hand, in order to come out on top, and assure a future for her son. Hagar looks for a wife for her son (v.21). She is typical of many poor Latin American women who, abandoned by their husbands, watch over and doubly protect their families.

God succeeds in instilling hope in Hagar. She revives. God opens her eyes (v.19a), and she becomes capable of seeing a well of water (v.19b). She fills her wine-skin with water and gives it to her son to drink (v.19c).

Ishmael will grow, according to the annunciation, and will be a "wild-ass of a man". Literally this signifies a savage human ass (16:12). That is to say that Ishmael will be one who will not be dominated, or domesticated, as his mother formed him. He will not be a slave like Hagar; he will be free in the desert, and a great archer (21:20). These were great qualities to the people of the ancient eastern world.[26] It would be a hard struggle for him to survive in the land between Egypt and Israel. People would laugh at him,[27] but he would never forfeit his right to life. "His

---

[25] Speiser, *op. cit.*, p.157.

[26] Von Rad, *op. cit.*, p.237.

[27] There is an Egyptian legend which makes fun of the bravery of such a Qadardi. The Egyptian editor surely uses it to ridicule the story of the Ishmaelites. Note the resemblance to the Ishmaelite descendant Qader. The legend tells of a fugitive from war who, full of fear, bumps into a wild animal in a clump of bushes in the desert. Testa, *op. cit.*, p.212.

hand will be against all, and all will be against him" (16:12), but he will succeed in erecting his tent before all his brothers. No one will be able to ignore him, and all will know the great injustice that was done to him and his mother in trying to erase them from history.

Finally, Hagar and her son will be free from Egyptian oppressors and Hebrew discrimination. They will be one with Yahweh, the Lord, through the rite of circumcision (chap. 17), and because of his name, Ishmael — God hears — for God will always be ready to help those in search of a new life.

The poor complicate the history of salvation. But God's action on their behalf teaches us that we should reconstruct this well-known history.

III. One Woman's Confession of Faith

Lee Oo Chung

"Why do you trouble her? She has done a beautiful thing to me. . . She has anointed my body beforehand for burying. And truly I say to you, wherever the gospel is preached in the whole world, what she has done will be told in memory of her" (Mark 14:6-9).

The story of the woman who anointed Jesus, which appears in different forms in all four gospels, is not all that often faithfully told — perhaps because we cannot grasp just what her preparing his body for burial meant for Jesus. But to read it is to wonder how it happened that women understood what Jesus said about his suffering and destiny while his disciples continued to miss the point.

Three times, Mark reports, Jesus tried to make clear to the disciples that he was about to die. The first is recorded in Mark 8:31. We read that when Jesus "began to teach his disciples, 'The Son of Man must suffer much... He will be put to death'..." Peter took him aside and began to rebuke him. But Jesus turned around, looked at his disciples and rebuked Peter: Get away from me, Satan.

Again in the next chapter: "The Son of Man will be handed over to men who will kill him" (Mark 9:32). How did the disciples respond? "They did not understand what this teaching meant and they were afraid to ask him." We can imagine that Jesus' stress must have shown in his face, making the disciples afraid to ask him about what he meant.

The third time is in Mark 10:32-33: "Once again Jesus took the twelve disciples aside and spoke of the things that were going to happen to him. 'Listen,' he told them, 'we are going up to Jerusalem where the Son of Man will be handed over to the chief priests and the teachers of the Law. They will condemn him to death...'" Again we see the disciples' alarm and fear.

What is occupying their attention? The sons of Zebedee come to Jesus and ask: "When you sit on your throne in your glorious kingdom, we want you to let us sit with you, one at your right and one at your left" (Mark 10:37). Already on the road the disciples had been arguing among themselves as to who was the greatest.

Their whole concern centred on their own glory, position and power — the exact opposite of what Jesus was trying to teach them. Even in Gethsemane, hours before his trial and execution, Jesus says to the disciples: "The sorrow in my heart is so great that it almost crushes me. Stay here and keep watch." But the disciples fall asleep.

Why did Jesus suffer so keenly? After all, he was the Son of God. Stories of many saints and heroes, ordinary human beings, tell how they died calmly and serenely. I believe the difference is that those saints and heroes bore only their own suffering, while Jesus took on himself the pain and suffering of all his neighbours, even of all humankind.

In Korea many women have had a son or a daughter or a husband taken by the secret police and tortured. When a mother or daughter hears how their legs or arms are broken, or of the internal injuries they suffer, her heart breaks. When she thinks of a loved one spending the winter in a cell so cold that many suffer frostbite, she cannot sleep in her own warm room. When she knows her loved one is underfed, perhaps to the point of death, she finds that good food almost chokes her. If sharing one person's suffering is this painful, how much more it is to share the suffering of all humankind!

Despite the pain, Jesus took on himself the suffering of all humankind. Yet his disciples did not understand, nor could they listen when he tried to teach them. Eager for glory and honour and power, they could not feel the pain of the suffering poor nor see the violence and evil of the oppressors.

In the National Museum in Kyungju, Korea, capital of the ancient Silla kingdom, is a beautiful bell. The Silla kingdom at the time enjoyed peace, but the king, a devout Buddhist, wanted to protect his people from foreign invasion. His advisers suggested that he build a huge temple bell to show the people's devotion to the Buddha.

A specialist in the art of bellmaking was commissioned. But despite his skill and care, he failed time and again to produce a bell with a beautiful sound. Finally, he went back to the council of religious leaders. After a long discussion, they concluded that the best way to give a beautiful tone to the bell was to sacrifice a pure young maiden.

Soldiers were sent to find and fetch such a young girl. Coming upon a poor mother in a farm village with her small daughter, they took the child away, while she cried out piteously: *"Emille, Emille!"* — "Mother! O Mother!" When the molten lead and iron were prepared, the little girl was thrown in. At last the bellmaker succeeded. The bell, called the Emille Bell, made a sound more beautiful than any other.

When it rang, most people praised the art that had produced such a beautiful sound. But whenever the mother whose child had been sacrificed heard it, her heart broke anew. Her neighbours, who knew of her sacrifice and pain, could not hear the beautiful tone without pain either.

Only those who understand the sacrifice can feel the pain. Others just enjoy the sound.

The salvation of humankind has not come through those who are comfortable and unconcerned, but only through the One who shared the suffering of all humankind. The woman in the gospel story, like many other women of her time, was discriminated against and oppressed, especially by the religious and cultural leaders of their society. Jesus understood and felt their suffering. Women must have loved Jesus very much for the way he related to them and shared with them as equals.

And so the woman in our story could understand the pain of Jesus, who was about to take upon himself all the pain of the suffering people. Jesus and the women knew that only where oppression, discrimination, pain and fear were shared would there be salvation and resurrection. That was why this woman poured the precious perfume on Jesus' head. Perhaps women are blessed with the ability to grasp the reality of suffering because they share and suffer more of the pains of history.

In the biblical tradition, pouring oil on someone's head announces that person as king or Messiah. So the woman's action is a confession of her faith: "You are the Messiah, the Son of the living God." The disciples were caught by a traditional concept of Messiahship as power, glory and victory. They could not free themselves from that image to hear what Jesus was trying to teach them of his messiahship.

But this nameless woman understood precisely what the messiahship would have to mean. That pleased Jesus so much that he praised her, saying: "Wherever the gospel is preached over the whole world, what she has done will be told in memory of her."

IV. Liberation, Theology and Women

Julia Esquivel

There are two biblical examples that illuminate the way the women of Central America are participating in the task of bringing about peace through justice.

One of these examples is the case of the prophetess Deborah. She held the function of governor or judge, at a time when the people of Israel had lost their way, had followed false lights and succumbed to idolatry. The leaders of Israel abandoned the true God, following the false lights of a deceitful and artificial world.

For twenty years life was unbearable for the people of Israel. Finally Israel begged God to help them. The leader of Israel at that time, the person who made Israel return to God, was Deborah, a prophetess of Lapidoth. She held audiences at a place which is now known under the name of Deborah's Palm, between Ramah and Bethel, in the mountainous region of Ephraim. The people of Israel came to her so that she could arbitrate for them and settle their disputes.

One day she met Barak, the son of Abinoam, who lived in Kedesh in the land of Nephtali, and she said to him:

> Jehovah, the God of Israel, commands that you mobilize ten thousand men of the tribes of Nephtali and Zabulun. Take them to Mount Tabor, to give battle to Jabin and his powerful army with all of its chariots which are under the command of Sisera. Jehovah says: "I shall lead thee as far as the river Kishon, and there thou shalt defeat them."
>
> I shall go if thou wilt come with me, Barak said to her.
>
> Very well, she answered, I shall go with you, but I warn you that the honour of defeating Sisera shall be that of a woman and not yours. Then she went with him to Kedesh....

The story continues, and tells us how God gave strength and victory to Israel against its oppressors. Of Sisera it is said that he fled and hid in the house of a woman called Jael. Jael received him, gave him water and when he was sleeping from fatigue she killed him.

When Barak came looking for Sisera, Jael came out and met him and said to him: "Come in and I shall show thee the man thou seeketh."

That day, say the scriptures, Yahweh delivered king Jabin of Canaan to Israel.

After the liberation war the people sing with their leaders. They praise the Lord thus:

> Hear well, kings and princes, because I sing to Jehovah, the God of Israel. When you made us leave Seir, O Jehovah, and guided us through the fields of Edom, the land trembled and the heavens poured down its rain. Yes, even Mount Sinai trembled before the presence of the God of Israel. In the days of Shamgar and Jael, the main roads remained deserted. The travellers used narrow twisted paths. The peoples of Israel remained abandoned until Deborah emerged like a mother for Israel. When Israel sought new gods, everything collapsed, our masters left us neither shield nor sword; among the forty thousand brave men of Israel not a single weapon could be found. How I rejoiced among the leaders of Israel!

There are some aspects of this that are worth stressing.

1. One is that even at that early period of history, during the period of the judges, God called on a woman to lead a people and to judge. She is the transmitter of the message of God to the man who is strong so that he, together with his men, may militarily defend the right to life and struggle for liberation.

2. Secondly, here it is shown clearly how God breaks through the mental and social constraints under which women suffer, in fact the entire ideology of the submission of woman to man.

The tradition of the strength of the male is broken. The captain of the armies of Israel asks a woman to accompany him into battle. And she who destroys the strong man of the enemy is a female fighter — Jael. She breaks a pact in order to defend the life of her people, its history and its future.

3. It breaks the tradition of submission and calls on us to place our bodies before the machine guns. It observes that we continue to talk instead of taking our liberation concretely into our own hands while thousands of our people are being massacred. It breaks through the false understanding of pacifism that masks the face of God, reducing God to ineffectual neutrality in the face of injustice and oppression.

Another typical passage illustrates women's political commitments to liberation in Central America in this very well-known text:

O how much I praise the Lord!
My spirit rejoices in God, my Saviour,
because he has seen the baseness of his servant
and henceforth the generations shall eternally call me blessed.
Indeed the All-powerful has done for me great things.
Throughout the ages he has been merciful with those who fear him.
How powerful is his arm! How he has scattered the arrogant and the proud!
He has humbled princes and has exalted the meek,
the hungry he has heaped with goods
and the rich he has sent away empty-handed.
And how greatly he helped his servant Israel!
He has not forgotten that one day he spoke to our fathers
and promised that it would eternally have the blessing of Abraham and his
    sons!

Before this song there is the statement by Elizabeth:

Blessed art thou for thou believest that which the Lord has told thee
and why this wonderful benediction shall be fulfilled.

These words have to do with the power of the faith that makes the
impossible possible. In order to struggle, in order to confront the enemy
who oppresses, courage, strength and devotion are necessary for these
alone make faith concrete.

In her canticle, Mary incorporates the experience of another woman,
Hannah, the mother of the prophet Samuel, a woman who gave her sons
to build the history of her own people.

The rural woman in Guatemala is capable of renouncing a life of
tranquillity in order to link her life with the historical destiny of her
people. For this reason, Mary is the typical image of the woman of faith.

The working-class woman and the professional woman have been
renouncing their normal future — a quiet family life and immediate
fulfilment — in order to join the struggle for justice and peace.

The sense of devotion, of total availability, of hope against all hope, of
faith which makes possible the impossible, which submits the only thing
one has — one's life — all this in order to collaborate with the future of
one's people, makes liberation possible.

Magnificat now
Sing we a song of high revolt;
Make great the Lord, his name exalt;
Sing we the song Mary sang
of God at war with human wrong.

Sing we of him who deeply cares
And still with us our burden bears
He who with strength the proud disowns,
Brings down the mighty from their thrones.

By him the poor are lifted up;
He satisfies with bread and cup
The hungry men of many lands;
The rich must go with empty hands.

He calls us to revolt and fight
With him for what is just and right,
To sing and live Magnificat
In crowded street and council flat.

                              Fred Kaan

V. Reversing the Natural Order

Marie Assaad

Every time I reflect on Luke 1:26-45, I realize how much it reverses all that we take as the natural order of this world and how God is still asking us today to reverse this order.

Here we learn about Mary, young and unknown, a woman in the patriarchal Jewish society, the poorest of the poor.

Why was she so highly favoured? Why did the angel Gabriel greet her in this manner? Isn't this a reversal of the natural order of this society?

Gabriel assured her that the Lord was with her. How often are we told that when we work with God, God will be with us! Is God truly with us? Don't we often waver in our faith? Even Mary was disturbed with this greeting. Why is she specially chosen? "I am a humble and weak woman. I have always been ignored. How can I suddenly get so much attention? And from whom — from Yahweh, the almighty, all-present, all-compassionate."

In effect Mary is told: "Although you are weak and have rarely received any attention; although you are used to work and toil in silence and nobody takes much note of what you say or do; although you feel you have so far only obeyed orders and listened to others; although you are not among the powerful and prominent, you have God's favour. Therefore, do not be afraid. Listen, and believe. God will give you a son."

"But how? I am not married. I am a virgin." Here we note the second reversal of the natural human order.

Everything is possible with God. "The Holy Spirit will come upon you," answered the angel, "and the power of the most high will cover you with its shadow."

What a task and responsibility! And what overwhelming news! She will conceive and have a baby. How will Joseph react to this news? Will he suspect her? Will he reject her? Will the world condemn her? How can she face the hostile world? Won't she be too weak to face all this alone?

Won't people gossip about her? Won't she be shunned by all, especially the women in her neighbourhood?

Yet, because she was used to listening and obeying, Mary did not argue or object. She said: "Let what you have said be done unto me."

Mary must have spent sleepless nights pondering over this visitation and its significance. "Why me?" she must have asked herself several times. How will I cope?

At dawn a still small voice must have told her: "Do not be afraid, Mary. Obey and I shall be with you, step by step."

It is with this deep conviction that the way will be shown her, step by step, that Mary decided to leave her home and travel alone from Nazareth to a town in the hill country of Judah, to Zechariah's home (not Elizabeth's, mind you).

Elizabeth's greeting affirms Mary's faith. With this show of solidarity from another woman, Mary's weakness and lingering doubts disappear. She is not suffering from hallucinations. This indeed is God's work. Not only is she chosen for a particularly difficult role, but she will be sustained at every step. The Holy Spirit is surely with her. How could she doubt? How could a child leap in a womb at the sound of a greeting? Is this natural? Here again is another reversal of the natural order. Yet, as Gabriel said, nothing is impossible with God.

Elizabeth was a modest, quiet wife, who had gone through years of grief because she had not fulfilled her greatest role as a woman and as a wife. She could not be a mother, and within Jewish tradition her existence had little meaning. She is getting old and her life has been futile. Yet Elizabeth, a woman, is filled with the Holy Spirit and declares, after the angel Gabriel: "Of all women, you are the most blessed, and blessed is the fruit of your womb. Why should I be honoured with a visit from the Mother of my Lord?"

Yes, blessed is she who believes that the promise made her by the Lord will be fulfilled. What reassurance! What a gift! How significant this was for Mary! How often do we need reassurance when we are challenged, or required to face difficult situations, or to carry heavy responsibilities! Is this what we mean by building solidarity among women?

With this assurance Mary feels liberated. She is liberated from her fears and misgivings, from her feelings of weakness and of inadequacy. She is liberated from what she was taught as a woman. Suddenly she sees the significance of Gabriel's message. She realizes what it actually means to be empowered by the Holy Spirit and how such power can reverse all so-called natural human order.

Then Mary, like Hannah before her, is filled with joy and gratitude and breaks out in a hymn of praise to God, her Saviour.

A humble young woman who suddenly discovers herself and what God can make of her, Mary offers the greatest song ever sung: the Magnificat. The song that is filled with the assurance that with God nothing is impossible. God can use us to reverse the state of affairs in our world of disorder, hunger and death, injustice, militarism, nuclear destruction. God can make us agents of shalom. God can commission us to prepare for a world where the lion will lie with the lamb and the rich will be accountable to the poor.

In this text God's option is not only for the poor, but also for women who are often the poorest of the poor.

VI. Living Stones

Grace Eneme

The image of "living stones" brings different images to different people, depending on their cultural backgrounds. I shall try to limit myself to my culture, trusting that the reflection will speak to others who share the same cultural heritage with me and to others who share my faith in Jesus Christ.

Among the Bakossi people in the forest region of the south-west province in Cameroon stones are classified into two main groups: living stones and dead stones. Living stones are stones that are movable, portable and usable. These include tripod stones, grinding stones, building stones, and many others. Dead stones are stones that are embedded in the bottom of the river, boulders and great rocks. These were hardly used till dynamite was introduced in the country.

Of the living stones, tripod stones for cooking have great significance to the Bakossi women. These stones serve a vital purpose in the life of the family and the community. Around them people meet for family discussions. Here is where moral instruction takes place and folk tales are told, a place of warmth and a refuge for strangers.

When a man takes a bride, one of the ceremonies which integrates her into the family is the laying of the tripod stones. The first stone is pitched by the bride and her husband, signifying oneness in building up their home.

The second stone is pitched by the bride and the eldest woman in the family, signifying her acceptance and integration into the family and village community. It also symbolizes her active participation in family affairs, mutual respect, and sharing with others.

The third stone is pitched by the bride and her chaperon (sister or aunt). It symbolizes a bridge of contact for the two families, the husband's and the wife's. By that stone the bride is assured solidarity by her family members in good and bad days.

From that moment on the stones assume their functions and the wife feels integrated in the family. Is the image of tripod stones the same as the image of living stones? Certainly not, but there is some similarity between them.

The image of living stones as presented to us by Peter signifies the church as a community of believers whose main function is service and witness. The community is compared to a building, having Christ as the foundation stone and Christians as stones in the edifice. As each stone is important in erecting the walls, so is each Christian in the community of believers. The appeal to build up Christ's church is an open invitation to all, male and female, young and old.

As the tripod stones integrate the bride into the family, so does Christ, the foundation stone, integrate each Christian into the family of God. Christ's family is bigger than any human family. It includes people of all races and colours, and it is bound together by his Spirit.

The call for integration into the family of God explains the universality of the Christian church. Never mind the denominational labels we carry. They are a mark of human sinfulness. How to put away our labels remains a problem to Christ's church because each denomination struggles to keep its identity and tries hard to build up its empire, often neglecting its functions in the society where it has been called to serve as living stones. This struggle hinders Christians from being open to each other or having meaningful supportive fellowship with each other.

Worse still is the oppression of women in Christ's church. Some church structures have laid down principles which are against women's development. They are happy to see women do menial jobs in the church and would like to keep them at that level. For others, the worth of women's organizations is measured by their economic importance and what they contribute to the general upkeep of the church and for supporting pastors.

Any programme aimed at developing women to know their worth and their place in church and society is often met with resistance from the church leaders.

Usually, the small group of women who stick out for such programmes are named "revolutionaries" and are sometimes ostracized by church leaders.

It is even more pathetic to see women themselves teaming up with pastors to discredit the so-called "revolutionary" women. Yes, we are a people groping in darkness. We need light but that light must come with great healing power. For decades we have been taught to be subordinate "little angels" and all the way through those social tapes play back to us.

In the family we are subordinate.

In the church we are subordinate.

In the offices, despite the laws and decrees made by the state to ensure equality, we are subordinate. No man would admit that a woman is equal to him, despite her qualifications. Christ alone assures us that we are not subordinate.

Christ was the only rabbi who did not discriminate against the women of his time. Since Christians have assumed the rights of Israel we share the rights which Christ gave the Jewish women. As he allowed Susanna, Joanna and others to minister with him so has he given us the full right and privilege to work with him. Since he is the Living Stone, our attachment to him makes us become living stones with him. While many Christians are dead stones, embedded in their old ways, while they fight for power and riches, we are called to be living stones and the pillars of that church which is being crushed by evil. This brings to my mind Father Balasuriya's theory "power + greed=evil". This evil has wholly permeated our churches. If there is hope for the church, it lies in the women, who are being "rejected" but remain the "cornerstones" of the churches.

All church women ought to unite and be in solidarity with each other for effective service in the world. We must congratulate our American sisters who have succeeded in creating an association of church women through which they can speak with one voice and witness to the world through corporate action.

We need a common voice and cooperative action to liberate our sisters who are exploited, be it by church structures, political systems or tradition.

It is most disheartening to see that women constitute a majority in most churches, yet in decision-making bodies they are only a decorative minority. In my church there are 17,000 women as against 6,000 men, according to the 1981 census.

In the African Protestant Church women constitute 85 percent of the membership. They are very active, contributing to the building of chapels and the maintenance of churches. They pay for the training of pastors. But in leadership, decision-making and the management of funds they have no part. Quite often the funds they provide are misappropriated by the elders and pastors.

In all these, it is evident that the rebuilding of Christ's church is in our hands. We have powers which we do not know! There is no great man in the world who did not pass through the nurturing hands of a woman, from birth right to the grave. We have the gift of intuition and the capacity for prompt action. Christ was aware of this, that was why he made women his first evangelists after his resurrection. His words "go and tell" mean that we should go and tell the broken church and the broken society what God is, what he has done for us and what he is capable of doing.

To prepare ourselves for this task, we must first of all know Christ. "Find out for yourself how good the Lord is, happy are those who find safety in him."

Knowing Christ is not a matter of theory. We have to experience it and allow that experience to become the basis of our existence. Only then would we know our worth and proper value and our obligations to church and society.

As a bride constitutes a bridge of contact between her family and the husband's family, so are Christians a bridge between the world and God.

Peter reminds us that we are a royal priesthood, meaning that every Christian is a priest. This statement is too difficult for us to understand. The tendency is to look at our spiritual leaders as all in all. And there is no doubt that some leaders enjoy being all to their flock.

What Peter is telling us is completely different. He is saying that our eyes should change direction. Instead of looking at the priest we should look at ourselves. As priests we are a bridge between God and our family, between God and our community, between God and our place of work between God and our church. In short, we are a liaison between God and all life conditions through our prayers of intercession and our service. We have to offer all our daily tasks with all their drudgery to God in our sacrifice of worship and praise. As we do this we dedicate ourselves to God and he gives us strength to move forward. We are not allowed to be static. Each new experience must bring us closer to God and the lives of those we are called to serve.

Building stones have one enduring quality. They can resist intense heat, rain, snow, frost, most of the normal climatic changes.

As women on the move in a changing society how do we see ourselves in the ministry? How far are we ready to go with Christ? Are we ready to take insults and shame? Nasty comments from friends and church leaders? Are we ready to be misunderstood, even when we are on the right path? Are we ready to spend sleepless nights, sometimes in tears, under the pressure of the discriminations we suffer and the concerns we cherish?

As living stones we have to resist it all through the power of the Holy Spirit. Looking up to Christ, our hope, our liberator, our captain, the road we must take.

> Sisters, power has been given to us by God.
> By the world's standards it can never be given to us.
> We have to struggle for it and grab it. So gird up your loins.
> Christ our liberator is our captain.

VII. Water in the Slums

Maria Teresa Porcile S.

A Bible story in Latin America

It was early in the morning, and cold — a harsh, dry penetrating cold. As soon as it was light some of the children in the district had to set out, hurrying on their way to a little school nearby. Daylight broke on a dirty bed with no mattress, no sheets, just a few ragged blankets that someone had once given them.

After a restless night it was time to go to school, without washing... you couldn't wash because there was no water. It was so early, and you had to go a long way to find a bucket of water... and there was no time. You had to leave right now if you weren't to be late for school. So you sat there, sleepy, without even having washed your face... would the teacher understand that you couldn't pay attention to your work?

It was early in the morning, and cold — a harsh, dry, penetrating cold. And Jesus said: "Give me a drink."

It was evening, and the day had been long and hard. The old man had spent the whole day trudging round with his cart, looking in dustbins, hunting through the refuse from the market... how little he had to show for all those hours, chased away from so many places, despised, never a kind word from anyone. And in the evening, back to the shanty-town, aching with weariness, back to the dirty bed, there perhaps to find a little companionship, an illusion of warmth. How good it would be to wash his tired feet at least, but where?... In the shanty-town there was no water...

It was evening, and the day had been very hard. And Jesus said: "Give me a drink."

It was mid-day and the sun was blazing down. It couldn't get any hotter. O for a cool drink of water... but there was none, and so in the group of men, someone produced a bottle of raw rum and the others began to help themselves, first one gulp, then another, and another... Suddenly tiredness seemed to recede, things seemed easier, reality less stark. Until all at once, someone let fly an insult he didn't really mean, but the result was immediate: curses, fists, fighting, knives, a wound, crime.

It was mid-day and the sun was blazing down...

And Jesus said: "Give me a drink."

It was mid-day and the sun was blazing down. It was very hot. Tired of looking for work they never found, the women never left the district now. There they stood at the door of their huts, surrounded by children, weighed down by the suffocating heat of the day after a sleepless night with their companions of the moment, drunk, bad-tempered... dirty.

And one of them saw her neighbour, that woman over there, the bitch, a harpy who had once stolen her man...

It was mid-day and the sun was blazing down...

And Jesus said: "Give me a drink."

A woman passed that way, coming from afar. She was a stranger, someone they didn't know and she carried a bucket. She went up to the well where the children were sitting, and the old people and the men and women, looking at the water in the well — the water, so near and yet so far.

And Jesus said: "Give me a drink."

And the woman answered: "Why do you ask me for a drink? You are poor and I am rich. You are thirsty but the bucket is mine."

And Jesus said: "Woman, what of the well? Whose well is it?" And the woman's eyes were opened and with her bucket they began to draw water for the whole district. The children could wash before they went to school, the old men could wash their feet after a day trudging round the rubbish dumps, and the men and women could refresh themselves in the heat of the mid-day sun... and, who knows, with a drop of cool, pure, clean water life might be a little easier, a little more bearable. Jesus said: "Give me a drink" and the woman who had a bucket and knew where a well was to be found, suddenly saw the spring, and she hurried to her own country, to her land and her friends and said to them: "Come, come with me and see something wonderful. I went to draw water there and, behold, I have found the spring which gives water of a different kind, living water. They say it springs when, at the well, those who are thirsty for life meet the poor who possess not even a bucket..."

And the thirst of the one and the bucket of the other make the water into something new and unique, a means of life-giving transformation in the human heart and in a whole district.

A Bible study method in Latin America

There are many different ways of doing Bible study. The traditional method is to take a text or a passage, situate it in relation to its overall context (cultural, literary, etc.) and then study the text itself for its deeper meaning, analyze it, explain the sense of certain expressions, words, particular phrases and, lastly, consider how it can be applied to our own lives and how it might change them.

However, there are other kinds of Bible studies which are perhaps not properly speaking "studies", but rather evocations of the revealed Word. These happen when we recognize an echo of some passage of scripture in an occurrence or event of everyday life. This is not to say that every detail of the contemporary event can be made to "correspond" step by step with the event narrated in the Bible, but nonetheless the one evokes the other as though calling on it for help in discerning the deeper meaning of the event or current life. This is what we have presented here.

What actually happened was this. In Montevideo, Uruguay, there is a project to develop contacts and solidarity between rich and poor in a middle-class parish and a slum area. The solidarity between the two very different social contexts has been demonstrated in many ways; communication and contacts between the two groups are developing well as the people get to know each other better. As we reflected on the theme of the Sixth Assembly of the WCC in Vancouver in 1983, as we thought of its theme "Jesus Christ — the Life of the World", we could see this event as a manifestation of life, expressed through water.

It happened like this: in the shanty-town there was one whole area which had no water; in fact nothing very much had been done about getting water, maybe because of a certain unconscious resignation on the part of the poor people who live there and who "have no voice". One day a woman who was working with the solidarity team in the shanty-town, though herself belonging to what might be called a bourgeois background, felt particularly uncomfortable, and in some definite way responsible for the fact that there was no water in the slums. She was married to an engineer who worked for the Public Works Department and she asked him how difficult it would be to provide water supply for the slum area. A fortnight later the shanty-town had its water. It hadn't been difficult, it cost next to "nothing", although "nothing" actually meant a considerable amount which the city charged for laying the pipes. But a collection was made in the middle-class parish and the pipes were paid for. The undertaking also involved willingness to run the risk of "paying the costs". But it shows what can happen when a person's heart and conscience awaken to the reality of poverty in a particular situation, and does so with a "new" sense of responsibility.

How can such an awakening come about? No doubt there are many "methods"; in this case it was preceded by a sustained encounter with the gospel, a living encounter with a living person. Communion with Jesus Christ who is the life of the world is the only thing which can reveal to us the meaning of the "parables" of life and death which are all around us. What is certain is that the coming of water into the district transformed the life of the community. Eight showers were built in a community centre in the area, and the character of the people changed. How can we fail to recognize in this story from a shanty-town in a modern Latin American city the deep meaning of water as a symbol of life? This event is an echo, an evocation of Jesus' meeting with the woman of Samaria (John 4:5-42). It evokes the biblical passage, it does not try to apply it or transplant it to another culture. It may be, for instance, that the similarities between the woman in our contemporary story and the woman of Samaria are very slight, but on the other hand perhaps we should all ask ourselves who are our husbands, "our masters", "our owners", "our idols", for we are all of us "women of Samaria".

However, what we are proposing here is an evocation, and it allows us to be as imaginative as we like. But we can hold on to the single central fact — the meeting of the thirsty man with the woman who had the means of drawing water. Simply that. And so, in John 4 and in our shanty-town, the fruit was the same: water of a different kind, and the people, all of them, gather round the Source.

VIII. Our Presence among the Poor

Priscilla Padolina

The text found in Luke 4:18-19 provides the basis for our Bible study. The words that I would like to lift up are:

Good News	poor
(release)	captives
(recover sight)	blind
(set free)	oppressed

Let us look at the context of this text. The setting is Nazareth, the place where Jesus grew up. It is a small place where everybody knew everybody else. Jesus was the son of Joseph the carpenter — that was his identity to them. As he stood up in the synagogue, he was handed a scroll of the book of Isaiah and he found the place where this text was written.

The text is significant because it is the announcement or proclamation of the beginning of Jesus' ministry. His being "anointed" refers to Jesus' baptism when he was affirmed the beloved Son. He was being conse-crated to fulfill the mission God had sent him to accomplish on earth.

It was clear that Jesus opted for the poor. He was deeply aware of the suffering of the poor from the injustices of his time. The ruling class had all the power; they were living off the poor and exploiting them. There was slavery, unemployment, high taxation, graft and corruption. The rich accumulated more and more wealth at the expense of the poor.

It was in this context that Jesus' ministry was announced: to preach good news to the poor. The central message of the good news is that human beings must be liberated from everything — and everyone — that keeps them enslaved. Life could no longer continue as it was. It was time that the poor, the captives, the blind, the oppressed receive life in its fullness, and enjoy life in a renewed and just society.

Who were the poor in Jesus' time? The beggars, the widows, the orphans, the outcasts. These were the rejects of society, the victims of oppression, people held captive. In his time Jesus mixed with these people and he was often criticized and despised because he was close to them. He wanted to show God's compassion for them.

What does this text say to us in our time? Who are the poor today? What comes to our mind when we speak of the poor? It is true that poverty is relative. What is considered poor in one situation may well be rich in another. In the developing countries, it is easy to identify the poor. In rural areas the poor are those who do not have basic needs such as water, adequate food, housing, education, health care. The poor are the malnourished ones, the illiterates, the women doing back-breaking work on the farms with crude implements, the jobless. They are the slum-dwellers living in dehumanizing conditions, the factory workers who work for a pittance. We should also include the tribal minorities whose lands are grabbed by the powerful, and the rural people who flee to the city looking for a brighter future but ending up in the slums, and often in debasing work.

What are the forms of oppression today? The situation is not so different from Jesus' time. Perhaps there is more sophistication in the patterns of exploitation and oppression. The structures of oppression are now better organized, institutionalized and internationalized. The domination of economic powers has become increasingly entrenched. The world resources and economy are controlled by a combination of social, economic, cultural and political mechanisms which are in turn manipulated by a few powerful sectors of society for their own benefit. Thus the gap between the rich and the poor has widened more than ever. And millions suffer in silence.

What is the good news that we can bring to:
— a landless tenant exploited by the landlord;
— tribal minorities pushed to the fringes of the country;
— the factory worker whose wages will not buy enough food;
— a woman who has to sell her body to survive;
— a political prisoner who is subjected to torture;
— women in captivity because they have to walk long miles for water;
— children brought up in the slums with no hope for the future;
— illiterate masses kept in the dark;
— blacks under apartheid systems;
— untouchables and unrecognized outcasts.

Going back to the key words in our text, the subjects there — the poor, the captives, the blind, the oppressed — are more or less in similar situations of suffering.

Good news is liberation, justice, empowerment, healing, love. It is also reflected in the active verbs: "*release — recover* sight — *set free*". It is restoring, healing the brokenness and dividedness in our world today.

How do we translate into action the good news that Jesus preached? How can we help liberate the poor? How do we empower the poor? What are the forms of oppression we should confront? Or do we also participate, consciously or unconsciously, in oppressing the poor?

Jesus opted for the poor. He knew and understood their sufferings. He took risks; he was rejected because he identified with them.

To participate in the struggle of the poor calls for a deep commitment to their cause. It calls for a profound understanding of their plight, their suffering, their aspirations.

Yes, it's bread we fight for
But we fight for roses, too.

They fight for bread in order to survive, but there is more to life than bread — it is the full recognition of their dignity as persons and as children of God that they want. These are the roses that give love, beauty, hope and meaning to their lives.

To participate in their struggles calls for an understanding of the root causes of their poverty and oppression, and learning from their struggles.

To participate in their struggles calls for our support in time of strikes by factory workers, in time of protests against unjust and inhuman treatment. To be in solidarity with them is to help raise their awareness of the root causes of their oppression. Education for conscientization is a slow and painful process, because we must start at the level where people are, raising their awareness on who they are, what they want, how they can get it, and whom they can count on.

To be in solidarity with them means to empower them. Jesus recognized the hidden potential in the people he met. The Samaritan woman was an outcast, but her life was transformed and she was empowered to tell her people about the Messiah. Empowerment is drawing out the gifts that lie hidden in people and helping those gifts to flourish.

There are two different philosophies of working *with* and working *for* the poor. The first one affirms and inspires self-confidence. The second often creates dependency and therefore more poverty.

To be in solidarity with the poor also means re-examining our own attitudes, our life-styles.

To be in solidarity with the poor involves risks. Women and men of faith in the history of the people of God took risks in participating in the struggles of the poor. In situations where structures are oppressive, confronting the structures and conscientizing the poor are considered subversive activities. Committed Christian workers are constantly being harassed by authorities.

The price is heavy if we aim to have justice and God's love reign so that all may have fullness of life.

IX. Birth

Mercy Oduyoye

At the age of sixteen I watched an eighteen-year old woman having her first baby. From that time I understood why an Akan woman was said to have returned safely from the battle-front when she had successfully pulled through that whole experience and returned with herself and her baby.

In this culture into which I was born, if news gets to a woman that another woman has not returned from this battle, she is expected to shake the words off her ears. They are not words that a woman should allow herself to hear — defeat at child-birth spells the presence of evil. Birth pangs should result in joy, not sorrow.

The new life is waited for with prayers, sacrifices and medicaments. But no material preparations are made for the expected child. No amount of that will ensure safe delivery of mother and child from this encounter between life and death. The mystery surrounding the arrival of life cannot be resolved or even minimized with busy buying of pink, blue and white ribbons. It is awaited with fascination and wonder and, above all, with prayer and right-living (i.e. observance of all taboos, mores and ethical injunctions of the community). The birth itself is in the hands of God. The woman, the bringer of new life, is at this point severely alone with her God and the hope of the new life. Others, especially the leaders of the family, are expected to be at prayer, calling all the relations in the other world to join in interceding for her. Others will stay by to encourage and guide but *the parting is between mother and child alone.*

The labouring mother, as Jesus observed, is at her most vulnerable and miserable, but her suffering is the prelude to the birth of a new life, a new beginning. As it happens, not all of us can enter into the experience of parting at this level.

Do you remember the last time you were faced with a decision to take a new job, or move into a new community, or even more aptly, when you faced expulsion from your own country and had to flee? Then you can imagine why babies cry when they enter the kind of atmosphere we have prepared for their reception. The baby girl I watched being born came into the world protesting vehemently. She was being given a rude shock; the established patterns of months were terminated in one sweep. The well-explored territory was exchanged for unlimited space of the texture of lifeless plastic and cold concrete. Imagine the insecurity that it will create. Remember Job — why on earth was I given to see the light of day? Our baby girl was not going to give up the comforts of the known without protest. The comforts of the familiar can easily make one complacent, and few welcome being shaken up and asked to wake up and live. And yet if the umbilical cord is not cut, the personal, responsible life demanded by God cannot begin.

To begin life as an individual, to become a responsible member of your community, you have to be able to decide where you want to be, and that you cannot do without suffering the pain and sorrow of parting with the tried and tested mode of life. To remain in a traditional mode does sometimes mean death. The security of the nursery has to be exchanged for the joys of achieving and contributing. Therefore Jesus said to Nicodemus, you must be born again.

When the baby finally arrived, I was disappointed. Is that all? She was neither beautiful nor cuddly; in fact, I did say that she was ugly. That is birth. But what potential! The mother smiles. "The ugly bundle" will be nursed into a beauty, with a pair of hands that may one day design cathedrals or perform experiments that will result in health for all. For the present at any rate, the labour pains vanish. God who mysteriously breathed the breath of life into her will supervise and direct that life. The chaos and darkness of the labour ward, the screams, sweat, swearing and the piercing cries are given a new quality. A new Adam has been stirred into life.

A living being in the image of God has emerged. Just as in Hebrew mythology, wisdom rejoiced most especially at the creation of human life, the whole community rejoices at this new addition to its task force. The physical agony had been borne by the mother alone, but not so the mental and psychological pangs. Therefore the birth of a healthy baby brings relief to the whole community.

The final discourse recorded by John is for me one of the moving episodes in the earthly life of Jesus and his disciples. In their place I would have been more puzzled than they seem to have been. Jesus promises them not only the sorrow of parting but the horrors of persecution. I have often wondered how much of the birth pangs image really got through to his male companions.

The birth image is for me basically that of parting, and the pain it involves. I understand that the Latin term used in medical jargon is actually the word *partum*.

First the separation of two lives that had got used to living together, with one depending totally on the other for its wellbeing, nay its very life. And yet without the separation at the appointed time neither will survive. Total dependence on God means life but total dependence on another human being is likely to mean the opposite. The separation between Jesus and his disciples was necessary if they were to be responsible grown-ups, telling the world what they had seen and heard. If the faith of the companions had remained parasitic on the faith of Jesus of Nazareth, the religion of total dependence upon God would have perished. He had to leave them.

The separation of mother and daughter or even mother and son is drastic and irreversible only in physical terms. In other respects they stay together, from childhood, through the puzzle of adolescence, and even into adult life. Death does not part them, for the memory of how mama used to say and do things lingers on. So does the presence of Jesus. I shall not leave you comfortless, he promised. Even when we, his disciples, do declare ourselves "come of age", we are honest enough to admit that we need the Holy Spirit now and always. We need to feel the presence of Jesus and to call to mind constantly the whole Christ-event. We need the assurance that he is alive and among us for evermore. The separation at birth gives independence but does not result in isolation and self-sufficiency.

The second birth image is located in the vulnerability and aloneness of the one who labours to bring forth a new life. It calls to mind Gethsemane and Calvary. The mythical bird, the phoenix, has to go up in flames to produce a new and unique successor and, according to St Paul, the old seed has to die to give life to the new plant. The cross symbolizes for me a new meaning of suffering. The new style of life ushered in by Jesus was designed to shake formalities out of religious life and to match belief with action. Such a radical perspective was not to be taken lying down. Those whose life patterns are threatened fight back. The protagonists of the new should therefore expect to suffer and not to be surprised if their suffering gladdens the hearts of those whose comforts they challenge. Once a baby is born the community cannot remain static, things begin to move to accommodate the new life. It is a fact that the early Christians suffered for daring to envision the birth of a new heaven and a new earth and for attempting to offer a foretaste of the life that is life indeed.

Thirdly, the new community was not the bouncing baby of postcards and greeting cards, but a weak and struggling group of not many rich, not many wise, not many saints — in fact, all were simply forgiven sinners struggling to live close to what they saw as the Christ-like life. Many unsavoury things did happen in the community of saints. The ugly phase of the infant church cannot be hidden. But Christians struggled on, believing that the Comforter whom Christ promised was guiding and would continue to guide.

The birth of Christianity was a community effort just like birth in an Akan family. One person took up the necessary physical suffering, but the whole community was supportive, indeed shared in the mental and psychological agony. The diversity of gifts came into play as some prayed and others prepared hot water. The communal suffering when it issues in the birth-event brings joy to all. The Christian community suffers with Christ as it struggles to share the work of Christ; caring for people in need is caring for Christ. It is a caring community that should issue out of the afflictions of the Christ.

In the Christian community, we are enjoined to practise the diversity of gifts, bear one another's burdens, do good to them that hate us. So the early church endeavoured to give birth to this new style of life. Persecution did not dampen their faith. Daily they prayed: Maranatha — Come Lord — and they did so even more fervently at the point of suffering. Why should they not suffer if the Christ suffered? At the point of death many saw Christ in glory and rejoiced that they would join him.

May this joy be ours.

X. New Testament Reflections on Political Power

Elizabeth Dominguez

Let us look at some passages in the New Testament with bearings on political power and the church.

The Magnificat — Luke 1:46-56. This is the song of Mary, the mother of Jesus, celebrating the fact that she is chosen to be the instrument of the incarnation. Here we find some clues as to how Luke looks at the state of political power in his time.

The relevant text for our purpose here is in verses 51-53, where we have the announcement of the incarnation which will deal with power. The purpose of dealing with power is so that the hungry will be given a new day. It's really that simple! But this is considered to be subversive because it has something to do with overthrowing rulers for the sake of the hungry. I do not know how you can read the text any other way. Power is not only questioned, it is even challenged.

To understand this more fully, let us look at 1 Samuel 2, from which the Magnificat is drawn, and then slightly changed to accommodate the theology of Luke. Here the idea of Hannah's song is that enemies are to be defeated — "the adversaries of the Lord shall be broken into pieces". In Hannah's song the king is going to be exalted and strengthened by God, but that is left out by Luke. Luke is very sceptical about kings and rulers. It is a very questionable set-up when you have kings and rulers, and comprehensive powers.

Herod — Matthew 2

The whole chapter 2 in Matthew is about King Herod, who felt so threatened when he was told that a "king of the Jews" was born. He had all the infants in his kingdom killed to make sure that this "king of the Jews" would be eliminated. Imagine Herod the King so threatened by a new-born baby. King Herod had such an unquenchable thirst for power, and, with it, a deep sense of insecurity. Power is a very strange commodity — the more you have it, the more you thirst for it and the more you want to grab it. Herod would stop at nothing to maintain himself in power. How many of us can look at chapter 2 in Matthew and then so easily quote Romans 13, where "all rulers are ordained by God"? Romans 13 cannot be quoted so irresponsibly as it often is today to justify state power.

So in Matthew 2 we are given a vivid picture of a tyrant — and the immediate implication is that tyrants are forces of wickedness working in every way to frustrate the plan of God, because of their lust for power. That is a very sharp criticism of government rulers. It is obvious that Romans 13 is talking about another kind of ruler. It cannot be a law that you just have to follow and obey regardless of who is the ruler — especially when the ruler is a tyrant drunk with power. You cannot imagine Herod as a ruler appointed by God! We therefore have the responsibility of deciding, when we look at our setting, whether Matthew 2 is the one that is to give us guidance in looking at political power or Romans 13.

Temptations — and the mandate of Jesus — Luke 4:1-21

Verses 18-19 are familiar. But I think there is some wisdom in considering the temptations in verses 1-13, which can clarify the meaning of verses 18-21, because the issue of the temptation stories is power.

The *first power* that was offered to Jesus was the power to turn stones into bread. Jesus turns it down. Why? Because turning stones into bread is done by those who do not really care for the people at the bottom who need bread, the poor. You can have all sorts of development, you can produce rice even for export — a way of turning stones into bread. There is a Japanese multinational which can turn cogon grass into something so useful that it could become more precious than rice. That is a miracle, but what kind of production is this? It is only show-off of power, to produce something out of "nothing", but for whom? Jesus would have nothing to do with this kind of power. You can master all the technology in the world, you can have all the signs that we really have progressed, but if the bottom, the marginalized of society is not at all benefited by this, then it is like turning stones into bread to prove that "I am powerful". Jesus says no to that.

The *second power* offered to Jesus was the power of a king. "If you worship me then you have everything, even all the kingdoms of the world." We have looked at the king and the state — the power that is comprehensive — power that you cannot escape from, especially in our time, because of the technology that can embrace all of life. And so Jesus has nothing to do with this kingly power either — it is not power for life.

The *third power* in the last temptation guarantees that if Jesus jumps from the highest point of the temple angels would hold him and he would come to no harm. What kind of power is that? Jesus said, No! It's the power to be immune from harm, never to be victimized, never to experience what the people are experiencing — whom we are supposed to serve. It is a power to be immune from feeling the pain and hurt of ordinary people, and so Jesus would have nothing to do with it.

And now comes the sermon of Jesus which quotes from Isaiah, "the Spirit of the Lord is upon me because he has anointed me to preach good news to the poor". The first sermon of Jesus characterizes his whole mission; it is his tone, his preoccupation and trade-mark. All the other powers in the temptations are not good enough to really serve the poor.

Look at what it involves to be poor and oppressed in the time of Luke — "He has sent me to proclaim release for the captives". How could this be achieved without challenging the illegitimate existing power? The wrong kind of power cannot fulfill the mission, and if you want to achieve your mission then it is inevitable that existing powers must be challenged. The captives in those days were mostly prisoners of war, the petty soldiers at the bottom who were captured. Even in the military you have those at the bottom being victimized, like the poor — and like the poor they are the ones to be given freedom.

In the text about the blind recovering their sight we see that blindness is a physical deformity that renders one heavily dependent, so that the potential of standing on one's own feet is lost. What you have as a gift from God has been prevented from operating. Any kind of dependency in which you cannot be on your own is a deformity, a state of blindness. Jesus talks about restoring sight to all kinds of blind people.

And he talks about "setting at liberty those who are oppressed". So often the oppressed are the weak whose weakness is used and manipulated in order to make them weaker and keep them in that condition. But the weak are to be strengthened and not manipulated. Think of the many things happening in our own society which fit this picture. Do we keep the oppressed permanently weak?

In conclusion, Jesus mentions the Jubilee Year when all prisoners are set free, debts cancelled, and you start anew — death and then resurrection — a constant happening when the old is surrendered and given up in every period. Releasing the captives, recovering of sight by the blind, setting at liberty those who are oppressed — all of these have to reckon with state powers and governments. It cannot be accomplished through charitable activities, by the kind of programmes that try to "help" without really getting to the root of the problem.

Rejecting the power of the gospel — Acts 4:1-22

Here in Acts 4 we have the rejection of power for another kind of power. After healing a man, Peter and John preach to proclaim the gospel. Healing is the fruit of the gospel. A very concrete human need is met. Something wonderful has taken place. But the rulers are threatened by this new power, they conspire to counteract what has just happened. They have difficulty, however, because the people are so happy with Peter and John. And what about the parallel in our own time? When you have a very determined force that is committed to work to change the predicament of the people, it is not welcome. You would think that anyone would say, it is good, this new thing, so let's avail ourselves of this power. But existing powers are threatened. This passage clearly and vividly shows how any good thing happening at the bottom is always assessed in terms of whether it is threatening the position of those in power.

Peter and John are charged by the rulers and warned not to speak in the name of Jesus, but they reply: "Whether it is right in the sight of God if we listen to you rather than God, you must judge, for we cannot but speak of what we have seen and heard." Finally the rulers had to let them go. They could find no way to punish them though they wanted to, because the people by receiving the gospel had also become a threat to the rulers.

This text is important because it shows how the early Christians, in being faithful to their mission, became a threat to the authorities. They were "subversive", which is how those who side with the poor are frequently called today. And Peter and John were not even questioning the rulers, they were simply preaching and healing. Later on we hear them declaring: "We must obey God rather than men." That was the formula of the early church. You have to make a decision, to obey God or man — and man here means rulers, oppressors. In our time we have some striking parallels. It might be relevant for us to be reminded of Matthew 10:20ff. and John 18:28 to 19:16, which show how state power operates — it has no conscience and no concern for truth or principles. Its main concern is to maintain peace and order at all costs. And then we have Mark 12:13-17, "giving unto Caesar", which is so often quoted out of context. Jesus very cleverly shows that he would not be trapped — that ought to guide us also.

Obeying those in authority — Romans 13

And let us look at Romans 13, where Paul the missionary is so frustrated with the church authorities. The key to understanding this passage is that Paul is also a Roman citizen. The Roman authorities have been good to him and saved him from many conflicts with the church. The rulers and the government here are definitely not a threat to those who are doing good. Paul was helped in his mission by government authorities, and so he is positive about the rulers. So Romans 13 should not be glibly quoted to justify any and every state power. Not all rulers are "ordained of God"!

Biblical faith is politically oriented

From these brief samples we can clearly see that the biblical faith is very politically oriented. The people of God always resist tyrannical power. The people of God must be vigilant of any political power. We have a lively tradition of protest throughout the Old and New Testaments. The primary context of the Old Testament prophets was one of confrontation with religious and political powers. The political powers must be constantly exposed for what they are, their deceptions and pretensions must be uncovered. We can support them only when they contribute to advance the mission of the church. And the mission of the church must also be carefully identified — it is about the birth of the people of God who become a community where persons are upheld for the building of community.

XI. A Letter to Job

Elsa Tamez

Dear Brother Job,

Your cries of suffering and protest have pierced our bones. We can't sleep. We weep tears of blood.

Your hands move in all directions: they signal to us, they enquire of us. Where are you taking us, brother Job?

The stench of death has penetrated our nostrils, we smell you everywhere. Your body covered with sores goads us. Pieces of your wormy flesh cling to our own. We have become infected by you, brother Job. You have infected us, our families and our people. Your eyes searching for justice have filled us with courage, tenderness and hope.

How brave you are, brother Job! How strong is your resistance! You are, like us, sick, abandoned, rejected and oppressed. Your friends Eliphaz, Bildad and Zophar haven't ceased to torture you and give you poor advice.

They say that you should suffer in silence and stop defending your innocence. They say that God has punished you and that you need to repent. And you, brother Job, in spite of everything, you haven't given up. Rather, your shouts have become louder. You don't believe them and you fight them. What's more, you dare to argue and wrestle with Almighty God. You blame God for your plight, and you accuse the Almighty of keeping silence in the face of your suffering. Once your friend, now God seems to have abandoned you. You don't understand why. You insist that you have been just and innocent. It is the right of every man and woman to cry out against unjust suffering.

Your friends have stopped being your friends because you have protested and because you have dared to touch the untouchable God. You have dared to touch the perfect God, the "Totally Other" who ordains the world without error and distributes justice left and right. But you don't see any sign of it. You see the suffering of the just and the innocent, and the happiness of those who exploit and pile up wealth. Your friends, with their well-reasoned speeches, affirm the contrary. It's they who should keep silent because you're the one who suffers injustice and experiences its consequences in your flesh and blood.

Let God answer! Let God explain his silences, his unbearable silences. How unbearable are God's silences! God's absence is like death. Our God, our God, why have you abandoned us?

Let God speak now and let your friends keep still, because God cannot be heard above their noise. Why don't your wise friends keep still? Their wisdom doesn't reflect the fact of life. They deny with words the pain and the suffering they see with their eyes. Empty theology! A theology closed on itself! A theology that tries to defend God with incredible lies! (Job 13:7). They defend God at the expense of human beings, instead of defending human beings in obedience to God.

Let them be quiet! Let them go back to the trash heap with you and let them weep and tear their robes for another seven days and nights. Let them identify themselves with you and your pain without speaking a word. Maybe in that way they will come to understand why the innocent have a right to protest and to rebel. Maybe that way they will be converted.

But let us be still as well, Job. Let's not complain any more. We have complained enough already. Your wise words silenced the wise of your time. They had no more arguments. God would not back them. Let the Almighty God stand before us and explain why for so long there has been such silence.

God's silence is mysterious. Sometimes it fills us with fright and paralyzes us in the face of the devils who squeeze out the life of the people. But without this silence of God we can't become men and women. When God speaks all the time, people become deaf. They don't hear the cry of the poor and of those who suffer. They become dull; they no longer walk and hope. They don't dare to do anything. They no longer endure.

God remains silent so that men and women may speak, protest, and struggle. God remains silent so that people may become really people. When God is silent and men and women cry, God cries in solidarity with them, but God doesn't intervene. God waits for the shouts of protest. Then the Almighty begins to speak again, but in dialogue with us.

God shows us how the mountain goat casts away her new-born and they find their way on the rocks and don't return looking for the mother's milk. God teaches us that the wild mule is free and that he laughs at the noise of the city. He doesn't slave for the mule driver but looks for his own food. The buffalo refuses to spend his nights in a stable; the ostrich scoffs at the rider of the horse who can't catch up with her; the horse neighs majestically and doesn't turn away from the swords of war; the eagle flies to the highest mountain top and takes in all the world with the sweep of his eyes. To all of these, God gave their strength and freedom.

Let's arise, brother Job, because you can't catch Leviathan with a fish hook nor the monster Behemoth with a smile. Only the strength of God in our strength can defeat them. The Lord challenges us; let's respond.

Now, brother Job, you have seen God, really come to know God. You will never be the same after this experience of suffering and after this vision of God. You'll never be again that rich gentleman who had all his wants and needs taken care of and who gave of his surplus to those who had nothing. You've had the intimate experience of being wretched and no one can erase this experience from your personal history. Now you know your God who is present with you and no longer absent.

God restored you because you wrestled with God until God blessed you. What will you do now? God restored you, but what of us?

Hope to see you again here in the trash heap struggling with us.

Elsa Tamez

XII. Two Christmas Stories

1. Born to her a son

Aruna Gnanadason

Mary carries the load on her head and climbs the precarious steps to the top of the building. "Hurry up, woman, I haven't got a year," shouts the contractor. She is just one of the many women he has employed. He is a building contractor. Mary carefully lowers the container with the cement, and for a moment stands holding her aching back. When will this long day be over, she wonders; when is she going to be able to lie down and rest? She does not tarry long, she is afraid the contractor will send her home; he was not too happy to employ her. No one has much use for a woman who is eight and a half months pregnant. Mary had got another day's work by lying that she is only six months pregnant. Thank heavens it does not show too much. She balances the empty container on her head and climbs down again. She controls a spell of dizziness and clings on to the ladder lest she fall.

Clutching the four and a half rupees she collects from the contractor, Mary rushes home. She has only recently started wondering why men at the construction site are paid so much more than the women. After buying some rice, onions and chillies, she stops for a glass of tea which she guiltily gulps down — this is a luxury she can ill afford. She wonders when this day will end as she recollects all the work to be done in the house.

Even from a distance she hears the wailing of her son and the angry voice of her husband who is trying to quieten him down. Biting back the rising irritation, Mary opens the door of their little hut. Her three children have been quarrelling over a banana which one of them had got from an old lady on the street. Joseph, her husband, unable to stand all their squabbling after his hard day at the carpenter's shop where he works, has beaten them all. While Mary's daughter sulks in a corner, the elder son looks back at his father defiantly, the little boy cries loudly. Everyone turns to Mary to bring peace to the house. She quickly tucks ten paise coins into the hands of the three children who run away, and Mary wonders when this day will end.

Joseph gives Mary five rupees out of his wages which she counts and puts away in a savings box to buy clothes for the children for Christmas — he takes away the other five rupees to the gambling hut... or maybe to the arrack shop. Mary starts the chores — the collecting of water, the washing of the clothes, the cooking of the simple meal. Sitting in the smoke-filled hut, tears fill her eyes. When will this day end, she wonders, when can she rest her aching back?

And so the days go on, Christmas draws near. The savings for the clothes never reach the cloth shop, they are given to the man who owns the land on which their hut stands. The threat of eviction hovers over them daily, monetary appeasement once in a way is the only way out. The houses of the rich, around the slum, are decorated gaily with stars and lights. The children look hungrily at the cakes, sweets, toys, clothes and firecrackers in the city's many stores. Joseph makes a simple star with bamboo and newspaper and hangs it in front of the hut.

* * *

As she climbs the ladder the load feels extra heavy, the backache becomes worse. The shouting of the contractor keeps her going. But a little later she just cannot continue. The uneasy feeling makes her rush home, and she gets home just in time. With the help of her ten-year old daughter, Mary delivers a baby boy. The women from neighbouring huts come in to help to make mother and child comfortable. A stray dog which roams the street, comes and peeps into the hut where there is great rejoicing. Joseph proudly looks on as people from the neighbouring huts move closer to see this babe that is born. The three leaders of the slum bring gifts — an old torn blanket, a bag of hay to make a bed and a glass of milk for Mary. The star that Joseph had put up welcomes one and all to that humble hut. Christmas is here; peace, joy and hope radiate from that unknown little slum, tucked away in a corner of that opulent city.

Mary's happy face looks down on her little son. The voices of children sing:

> Away in a manger, no crib for a bed
> The little Lord Jesus lays down his sweet head.
> The stars in the bright sky look down where he lay,
> The little Lord Jesus asleep on the hay.

Mary looks at her little son and tears of joy well up in her eyes; the little babe is a symbol of hope to her. She remembers the construction site, the low wages, the empty savings box, the fear of eviction, the unsure future. To her the baby seems to be saying: "Why woman, why do you humbly and passively acquiesce in all this which oppresses you? Get up and resist — you are the woman of the Magnificat." And Mary smiles, for today is born to her a son.

2. The beating of a young heart

Mahat Farah El-Khoury

On the radio the voice of Fairuz, the popular Lebanese singer, was heard singing "The Night of Christmas".

Mother and father had just returned, fatigued after a long day of work. The four children were impatiently waiting. What were they expecting? A Christmas tree? Beautiful gifts? A special meal? Were they expecting all these together, or nothing?

Food is served, the usual meagre meal. The family income is hardly sufficient for a family of four. Asma'a, the eldest, a girl ten years old, is listening to Fairuz with tears in her eyes. She is holding a pen in her hand, trying to write something.

"What are you writing, Asma'a? Are you copying Fairuz's song?" asked the mother with concern.

"No, mother. I am writing a letter, rather a Christmas card, requesting an explanation, or perhaps expressing a reprimand to 'Santa Claus', or rather to Jesus Christ." Asma'a continued: "You adults send Christmas cards to family and friends, but I send mine to Jesus of Nazareth. I wish to address the Son of Mary; I want to talk to him. I wish to tell him about what is happening on earth, for he is far away, very far away. Perhaps he has not heard. I shall hurry to place the letter on the reading altar for the angels to carry it to him. Perhaps he will hear, perhaps he will respond."

The mother was amazed, and kept asking herself: "What has happened to my daughter? Has something gone wrong with her mind?" Then she was busy with her housework, leaving her daughter with her writing.

A little later the worried mother went back to find her daughter finishing her letter. She picked it up and read:

"My beloved Jesus,

On the occasion of this blessed Christmas, the day of your birth, I come to you because I was taught: 'Let the children come unto me and do not keep them away...' and since I am one of these children, I have decided to come to you. If not in body or voice, I come to you through my words. Glory to God in the highest, peace on earth, and good will towards people. Thus did the angel sing on the night of Christmas. Glory in heaven, yes, but on earth... war, killing, misery and pain.

They came to you on this blessed night with gold, frankincense and myrrh. Today they use gold to manufacture destructive weapons, or buy them. They feed the good people with bitter herbs. As to frankincense they burn it for criminals and murderers.

Around your cradle were sheep and goats; it is today surrounded by wolves and crows.

Love is your symbol, Son of Mary; but where is love? It has become an empty word, ink on paper.

They taught me that you came to save humanity. Humanity is now drowned in the abyss, in evil, in darkness and destruction.

You said: 'It is easier for a camel to enter the eye of a needle than for a rich man to enter the kingdom of God.'

Here is the rich person, wherever he is, entering palaces and villas, rising up to the sky in airplanes, flying with his wings everywhere and strutting about like a king. Before him the people bow low in fear.

You said: 'My sheep hear my voice, I know them, and they follow me.' Your voice rings in our ears, O Son of Mary, but your sheep ignore your voice. They are too busy for you. They do not follow you. They walk behind the false, the trivial and the mortal. Come again. Perhaps you could reform humanity, and straighten its crookedness. Come to spread your message; the message of love and justice, of brotherhood and sisterhood. Finally, I kiss you, wishing you a happy Christmas. Till we meet soon on earth, or in heaven,

Little Asma'a"

The mother read the letter, and her thoughts were carried to Jerusalem, to the prisons and concentration camps, to killing and destruction, to wounded Lebanon. They were carried to the wounds made by those who profess faith, to those who burn and destroy in the name of religion...

Tears fell from her eyes, and she said: "Hurry, my daughter, hurry and deliver the letter. Perhaps it will reach him, perhaps it will bring about the desired results."

Part II

New Eyes
for Seeing

I. Woman, For How Long Not?

Bette Ekeya

In this article, I am going to reflect on the fact that, although Jesus' Good News has indeed been preached to my people, one section of these people remains poor, captive, blind, down-trodden and unaware that the Lord's favour rests upon them. This group is the African women. The coming of the missionaries, about a century ago, should indeed have been very good news to the African woman, but now, besides the cultural norms and taboos that bound her and held her in subjection, two other oppressive elements have been added to her world: the loaded interpretation of certain biblical passages and the predominantly male church ministries and institutions.

The African culture

Rather than generalize on African culture, in this section, I will give a brief description of the life and social position of the woman among the Iteso, although most of what I am going to say can be applied to the African woman in general.

The Iteso live in the Teso District of Uganda and in parts of the Bukedi district of Eastern Uganda. They are the second largest ethnic group in that country. A small group of the Iteso of Bukedi district were cut off from their Ugandan kin by the colonial Kenya-Uganda border. The Kenyan group is a very small minority. Christianity was preached to the Iteso by the Mill Hill missionaries of St Joseph and by the Church Missionary Society. The Kenyan Iteso are predominantly Roman Catholic. I will confine my remarks to the impact of Roman Christianity upon the Atesot woman.

The Iteso whom the early missionary encountered were a people who believed in one God called *Akuj*. This Akuj was believed to live *kuju* — far above in the sky. *Akuj* it was who created the world and all people and continued to take care of them. Akuj could be invoked at any time, anywhere, when the need to invoke him arose, although in times of national crises communal prayers and sacrifices were offered. On these occasions, religious specialists called diviner prophets-cum-priests, officiated. The religious life of the Iteso people was not confined to special religious times, however; rather, as with all African peoples, religion permeated all of life.

One aspect of Iteso religion which largely concerned women was what was called domestic rituals. It was in the domestic sphere that woman's life was concentrated. The highest aspiration of an Atesot woman was to marry and have children. Towards the fulfilment of this, she was carefully raised and trained. Her father made a careful choice as to who should marry her when she came of age.

The marriage of a young girl was a painstaking affair which stretched over a period of time, a gradual undertaking which consisted of several stages. Two extended families or clans participated in it: the future husband's clan and that of the future bride's father. It was a covenant of two communities whose external symbol was *Asuti*: that is, the transfer of an agreed-upon size of livestock from the family of the boy to that of the girl. *Asuti* legalized the marriage and helped to guarantee its success and stability.

Marriage for a young Atesot girl meant leaving her father's homestead, abandoning her father's clan rituals and going to live in a strange home with strange clan rituals. It was a major transition in her life, and to ease her passage from one state of life to another, more complex one, she went through rituals of incorporation. These rituals initiated her into the married state and incorporated her into her husband's clan. There were the rituals of anointing her with the oil of her husband's clan which was her wedding ceremony, her ritual introduction to all the various domestic chores she was henceforth to perform, rituals accompanying her first pregnancy. At the successful birth of her first child, rituals were performed to welcome her child into the community and at the same time cleanse her from the process of childbirth, which had rendered her ritually unclean. With the birth of her first child, the young girl ceased to be a child and became a mother. More rituals were performed to mark this transition. Other rituals were performed to ensure the health and survival of her children.

Apart from incorporating her into the clan of her husband and into the married state, the rituals which an Atesot woman underwent and participated in were also designed to give her the necessary spiritual strength, and protection against the myriads of malevolent spiritual forces with which the world was believed to be inhabited. Some of these forces operated in the form of spiritual possession and in witchcraft, sorcery and evil magic. Children were especially vulnerable in the face of these forces, and so the woman needed rituals which she could perform to ward off these forces from herself and from her children. Except in cases requiring the special intervention of healing specialists, these rituals were organized and performed only by women. The young woman learnt the significance of the various rituals as she learnt to grow and operate in her new state and in time she too became a specialist in performing them for the wives of her sons. No man ever dared to legislate, discuss, change or officiate in these domestic rituals. This was where woman was supreme.

Iteso society, like African society in general, treated woman with an accepted cultural dichotomy. As long as she was the mother of healthy children, sons and daughters proportionately, her place in the home and in her society was assured and honoured. Both her father's clan and that of her husband did everything possible to make her marriage work. She could not be arbitrarily dismissed or divorced, for the legally married woman always belonged where she was initially married. She could go *ekurumane*, that is, be "held", be "married" somewhere else, but should she wish to return, the cultural laws obligated the first husband to take her back. Polygamy was an accepted form of marriage and all wives in polygamous marriages were legal wives.

Outside of the home, the woman had no real influence on society. Her rights were never equated with those of the man. While still in her parents' homestead, it was her father and brothers who had almost absolute rights over her. Her husband was chosen for her, her marriage was necessary to bring her brothers the bridewealth which would eventually become the *asuti* for their wives. It was the man who married her. She it was who gave up her clan taboos to adopt those of her husband, and henceforth she became identified with his people. Children were always members of their father's clan. In the event of a marriage breaking up, the woman was never given custody of the children. When children turned out well, her husband got the credit. When children grew up into bad characters, the fault was wholly their mother's. Should her marriage remain childless the fault was hers alone. A childless woman was perhaps the most miserable of women.

In every period of her life the Atesot woman had to live in the shadow of a man. Her existence was defined and given legal sanction by men. It was marriage and motherhood which gave her complete fulfilment as a person. The single woman, fully self-sufficient, was an anomaly. It was considered an abnormality and a curse for a woman to remain a resident of her father's homestead all her life. Such a decision on her part was believed to bring ill-luck to her father's homestead. When her husband died, she could not inherit his property. If she was a young widow, her husband's next of kin inherited from her. If she was past child-bearing, she could elect to be housed and fed by one or another of her married sons.

Within traditional Iteso society, woman lived quite a happy and contented life because there was nothing to challenge the cultural norms under which she operated. Then along came Christianity with its promise of the Good News of salvation. Missionary Christianity came to the Iteso in the form of Roman Catholicism and Anglicanism (CMS), both very traditional and rather conservative, particularly in their understanding of morality and in their understanding of the place of woman in society in general, and in particular in the Christian community. The "Good News" which missionary Christianity brought to the African woman was more in the field of education than in spiritual transformation. It is indeed true that Jesus Christ has been introduced, but the Good News that the person of Jesus Christ should be and wants to be for the African woman remains hidden from the majority of them. The minority who have encountered Jesus Christ in the manner of the New Testament women (like the Samaritan woman, John 4:2-11), the woman caught in adultery (John 8:2-11), the woman with the hemorrhage (Luke 8:40ff.), for example, are those women who are "saved", in religious life, in good Christian marriages and in canonically recognized lay organizations. These can claim to have encountered the Christ who, notwithstanding the existing cultural and religious laws that forbade any public communication between women and rabbis, reached out to women who had been declared social outcasts and gave them new hope and the feeling of wellbeing.

Two main reasons may be examined which hinder women from personally meeting Jesus Christ fully: the way certain passages of scripture have been and continue to be interpreted to the detriment of women, and the predominantly male-oriented church ministries and institutions.

Interpretation of certain passages of scripture

One teaching which has hurt a certain percentage of African women and placed them outside the salvation community is the interpretation of Matt. 19:4-6. This passage presents Jesus' interpretation of marriage as divinely instituted and monogamous (cf. Gen 2:18-24). Iteso men who wanted to become Christians were told to send away their wives and choose only one with whom they could contract the sacrament of matrimony. Iteso traditional marriage, which was culturally legal and binding, was not recognized by the church. Those unfortunate women who were not chosen to become Christian wives were declared concubines and their children bastards. The once happily married women found themselves abandoned and homeless. They could not return to their fathers' homesteads. Some were no longer women in their prime who could be married again.

For a while, this strategy seemed to work. Those who adhered to the form of marriage which the church insisted upon were those whose livelihood was dependent on missionary employment. For a man employed by missionaries to take another wife was to risk his job. When, later on, the government took over the task of employing most people, many men in monogamous marriages became polygamous. Currently, the major factor that is making polygamy difficult is the high cost of living. The majority of marriages contracted by the average Iteso of the rural area tend to follow traditional marriage lines, even when they are not polygamous.

Another church teaching which has served to emphasize the subservient position of women is the interpretation given to Col. 3:1a and Eph. 5:22a: "Wives, be subject to your husbands." What is implied in Eph. 5:21 "Be subject to one another out of reverence for Christ" is usually ignored or down-played. The fact that men should love their wives with a sacrificial love is hardly ever highlighted. By emphasizing woman's subjection to man in marriage the church has directly given men the excuse for laxity and tyranny in their dealings with their wives. Laxity here is the tendency men have of being unfaithful to their wives. They are of the opinion that women should be faithful because they must be submissive to the men. Women are expected to practise a higher morality than men. Women have been blamed for their husbands' unfaithfulness; for, the argument goes, if a man goes after other women then the wife must be lacking in some way. This argument is too one-sided. It does not take into consideration the fact that in marriage, frustrations, lack of fulfilment, be it sexual or personal, could be caused by either the man or the woman. Of course no man could ever tolerate his wife's unfaithfulness because it is considered a direct affront to his authority.

The church's emphasis on the subjection of the wife to her husband in marriage has given many men an excuse for being tyrannical to their wives, even to the extent of physically assaulting them. It is of course natural to discipline one who is one's subject and the subject is expected to accept the discipline as part of her position. In marriage, as the church presented it to our people, woman is the subject who can and often should be so disciplined. The fact of the complementarity of the man and woman in marriage has not become an integral part of the teaching of the church. In a very subtle way the church encourages woman to endure the hardships of marriage even to the point of accepting an impossible marriage relationship as a necessary martyrdom.

Traditional Iteso society had provisions for preventing excessive cruelty to wives. A court of elders often met to settle serious cases of incompatibility in marriage. Church marriage has no such provisions, especially with its emphasis that marriage is an affair between two parties only. Always there is the underlying view that it is woman's lot to suffer in marriage because the Bible says so (1 Tim. 2:14; Gen. 3:16). Was it not the woman who, after all, brought evil and disorder in the world by her sin? She should therefore take what life metes out to her and accept it as part of her atonement for causing man to sin. Often this interpretation of the story of the Fall is taken literally, with complete disregard of the historical and cultural setting of the story. The revolutionary interpretation to it which Jesus gave by his own example is quite ignored.

Jesus Christ had every reason to perpetuate the subjugation of women. As a Jewish rabbi, he must have been aware of the practice the male Jews had of thanking God each day that they were not created slaves, gentiles or women. But in his own relationship with women, he chose to ignore the traditional Jewish attitudes and instead treated women with compassion and complete acceptance. For his pains he earned the reputation of being the friend of sinners. To those women who encountered Jesus of Nazareth in his life-time, he must have been really Good News.

These interpretations of the Bible have only confirmed to the woman that her apparent low status is in accordance with the divine will and the natural order from the beginning. When Christ's relationship with women is discussed, and whenever related passages are expounded by preachers, Christ's own full acceptance of women is discussed in very low key. A sermon on the woman who washed the feet of Jesus with her tears manages to ignore Christ's love for the woman as a person and instead concentrates on her abject sinfulness. Christ is portrayed as pitying women as morally weaker vessels, for after all if he fully accepted them as equal with men why did he not include them among the twelve apostles? The story of Mary, from whom seven demons had been cast out, as being sent by the risen Christ to announce the Good News of his resurrection to his brothers is invariably ignored. But she was the first apostle of the resurrection.

Church ministry

The ministry of the church is a predominantly male enterprise. Only men go through ministerial training and only men get ordained as priests. The ministerial training which priests undergo removes them culturally and physically from the people they are preparing to minister to. By the time a man completes his training he has become a stranger to his people. The people regard him as someone outside and above their ordinary lives. Very often he has no way of touching the lives of the people.

During their priestly training, one over-riding indoctrination is in the area of sexual morality. Moral decadence becomes equated with having any kind of intimacy with women. Sexual abstinence or celibacy is regarded as part and parcel of priesthood. The future preachers of the Good News of Christ's salvation are warned in no uncertain terms to avoid women. Woman is portrayed as the archenemy of a priest's holy vocation. Women are to be treated objectively and formally. Young women are to be especially shunned because of their terrible power to confuse the heart and head of a young man. Sermons have been preached from the pulpits on Sundays which castigated young girls who dared to have anything to do with seminarians. African priests leaving the seminary are generally quite ignorant of how to approach women as persons. They feel safe with religious and married women but are at a loss with young unmarried women. Should a priest seduce a young woman, his sin is nicely covered up by his bishop while the young woman is as good as tried, condemned and executed, psychologically and spiritually.

The traditional woman had her domestic rituals which sustained her. Missionary Christianity, combined with inevitable cultural changes, has tended to belittle, if not prohibit outright, the performance of these rites. They were dubbed demonic or superstitious. Their spiritually healing power for the woman whose whole life was full of special difficulties was never fully appreciated. No alternatives were given and consequently a vacuum was created which has never been filled. For example, whenever there was serious illness, especially psychosomatic illness, a woman could go to a traditional healer who was very well versed in diagnosing such illnesses. These healers prescribed a healing ritual which usually involved a healing of relationships, for this was the common cause of such illnesses. After performing these rituals of healing, the patient was cured.

The church has no real effective healing ministry which corresponds to this sort of thing. The coming of Christianity and Western civilization has caused an upheaval in the world of the African woman. Her way of life was disrupted if she had contracted a polygamous marriage. Christianity condemned the traditional healers as diabolical. It condemned all of African culture as pagan. The African had to adopt Western ways in order to become a Christian: naming ceremonies, dressing and etiquette, education, recreation and even burials — all had to be "Christian".

The tensions caused by these changes are considerable. Christianity did not remove the African from the African world, which conflicted with the new world of Christianity. The ministry of healing was often confined exclusively to physical ailments. Hospitals healed the body but often left the spirit and psyche ailing. For spiritual healing, one could go to a priest, but the priests did not understand the psychosomatic illnesses that troubled people, particularly women. Few women ever feel free to consult a priest.

There is an increase in the number of African women who find themselves unmarried and outside the convent. Most of these women are educated and professionals in their chosen fields. For one reason or another they could not conform to the kind of life which society defines as acceptable. Many of them would have wanted to give their lives to the service of the church, but the church, as already pointed out, does not readily welcome them in ministry. A great many of these women find themselves in the very difficult position of single motherhood, widowhood, broken marriages or in unfortunate liaisons with men. It should be a very natural thing for a single mother to find welcome acceptance in the church; instead, their state of single parenthood is considered a permanent state of sin. Having fallen before, they are given little or no encouragement to get up and live among persons who understand and are morally supportive. If anything, fingers are pointed at them as persons who must be avoided and whose terrible example must not be imitated. A man who sins and then confesses is more readily forgiven and accepted than a woman who, out of loneliness or weakness (or cleverly seduced), finds herself a single mother.

The single woman faces the terrible ordeal of becoming a social misfit. She risks becoming turned in on herself. It is extremely difficult for such a woman to get the seemingly necessary spiritual guidance of a priest: few priests can appreciate the life of a single woman, and frequent visits to a priest, however innocent they may be, will be misconstrued. These women find it difficult to encounter the Christ who came to give liberty to captives. In their lonely struggle to cope, they often cannot experience Christ as a person who cares for them.

For the majority of African women, the Good News which is the person of Jesus Christ is still inaccessible. Unless church structures radically change and allow women to receive the liberty which the Son of God died to make available, there can be no real transformation of people's lives.

II. Churchwomen and the Church's Mission

Mercy Oduyoye

"Look to each other's interest and not merely to your own" (N.E.B. Phil. 2:4).

This is primarily a study of the concept of sacrifice from the perspective of Christian theology. It is informed by my experience of women's lives as a "living sacrifice". In trying to understand this, I have concentrated on the church's mission in Africa, focusing on what has been done and what needs to be done.

In talking about churchwomen, I do not wish to get into ecclesiological questions, but simply to state that the term "church" will be used to stand for the whole visible body of organized Christians in all the confessional families, communions and denominations functioning in Africa (and elsewhere). It will include the "charismatic churches" of Africa, i.e. Christian communities that have come into being through the evangelistic activities of Africans who have been moved by the Spirit of Christ. These are currently designated African Independent Churches.

The community which Christ called together, and which became the embryo of the church, included women. There is no record of a special decision of Christ to call women to become part of the church, but there is in Gospel records firm foundation for the assertion that from the beginning women belonged to the church of Christ. Since I do not see women as outsiders who "come into" the church to "play a role" and then withdraw, I do not want to speak of "women's role in the church".[1] By churchwomen I mean all believers who, as disciples of Christ, seek to or have become promoters of Christian ideals, and who by the will and in the wisdom of God fulfill the biological necessity of being female. Like

---

[1] Amba Oduyoye, *And Women, Where Do They Come In?* Lagos, Methodist Publications, 1977.

churchmen some churchwomen are stipendiary and others are not. Some belong to the "representative ministry" of the church, while all belong to the church's general ministry according to the charism that they have received.[2]

Sociologically churchwomen come from all sectors of society and from all walks of life, professional, vocational, academic, celibates and parents. Organized or singly, women are those who take their membership of the body of Christ seriously by virtue of baptism and who feel called to serve the church, "to minister" as well as "be ministered unto". Being an integral part of the body of Christ churchwomen like churchmen are called to "play a role" in the world, their presence is always manifest beyond doubt. Even in a situation when one is unable to physically separate the church from the world their presence is never lost as the effects of it are perceived by all.

The mission

Jesus called people to become involved in the announcement of the rule of God in the world. The church's function is to make this fact known, and to be first-fruits and represent the shape of a human community when it is fully submitted to the will of God. As a visible body of believers, the church is called to a priestly function, the dual role of representing the world to God and God to the world. It is called to be a sacrament and a sign of the kingdom of God.

In fulfilling this assignment, the church may lose itself in the world but in Christianity life lost for the sake of Christ and the kingdom is life regained or renewed, for it is bound to be transformed as it transforms the world. The church is in the world to announce, proclaim, and live the kingdom and to do so with all forthrightness. This prophetic function is exercised not only with words that hang in the air or simply become a part of the reasoning and conversation of people, but words that become incarnate in deeds. The church is called to be the bearer of the New Humanity like the mother of our Lord.

The manner of executing the mission cannot be separated from the mission itself. It is in this respect that I wish to situate the Christian's call to self-denial, forgoing privilege and embracing a simplicity of life whose wealth is not only in being poor-in-spirit but in being a church of the poor for the sake of the kingdom. The style of mission is to be the style of the

---

[2] "Baptism, Eucharist and Ministry", *Faith and Order Paper No. 111*, Geneva, WCC, 1982.

Christian bride who intends to live in mutual obedience with a loving husband in a household whose head is Christ. The church's mission is to be undertaken in the spirit of a Pauline wife who says nothing in public and lives according to the modesty demanded by the norms of the community, fully assured that she reflects the relation between Christ and the church.

My question then is, does the church in Africa take all this seriously? The church cannot question the love and wisdom of God in the same way as a woman who may have every reason to question the integrity of the man she is expected to obey. We cannot doubt that life in the kingdom will be our highest glory, in the way that women have had reason to doubt whether the "standard" of humanity experienced in masculinity has resulted in the best ordering of life, i.e. that norm of living which is close to life under God. The yardstick of Mark 10:42-45 will meet only a negative response in that context. The Lord, in the exercise of authority, goes to the point of giving up his life that many may be freed, and that is not true of us.

The church, like a bride, has signed on to be integrally part of a costly enterprise which demands forsaking all and denying self for the sake of the glorious life of the kingdom. Christians are those who have opted to be involved in God's work of transforming the human community into a people ruled by God. Unlike women in their role as wives, the church is totally assured of the love of God and may therefore confidently proceed in this enterprise in the spirit of total dependence upon God. Unlike a woman the church is assured that losing itself in the life of Christ (being in Christ) is the only way of being truly the church. There are therefore no ifs and buts around its call to live the "truly human" life — which in the human ordering of community is demanded only of women. It is the whole church that is called upon to sing with Charles Wesley "Behold the Servant of the Lord".[3] Hence the woman becomes the model of the church, and the discipleship of Mary the mother of Jesus and "the other women" become examples not only for churchwomen but for all Christians.

On earth the church is on a mission, and Christians see themselves as a people who have been sent by Christ. Being sent always means forgoing one thing in order to undertake another, and therefore involves dedicating, consecrating, and setting apart or aside, indeed giving up much so that the new mandate may be fulfilled. Thus Christians individually and corporately as the church are called to a life of sacrifice.

---

[3] British Conference, *The Methodist Hymn Book*, 1933, No. 520.

Sacrifice

Since in every age and place, the concrete tasks entailed in being called of God take on different shapes and intensity, I intend what I say to be heard in the context of contemporary Africa and therefore wish to call attention briefly to the function of sacrifice in the practices of "primal religion" in Africa. In this way we shall be able to situate the sacrifice of churchwomen in Africa.

As a religious practice, sacrifice is central to the primal world-views of Africa, marking as it does the religious feeling of dependence upon a reality that is beyond the normal experience of humanity. Thus when a community encounters a crisis that threatens the fullness of life, a sacrifice is called for, and women are often the most eager to see them through as their "main concern is first and foremost the domestic wellbeing" as Ezeanya says. Speaking of Igbo women he said:

> They often consult diviners who may prescribe sacrifice. In this case women will quickly make the necessary contributions in money or kind and meet the priest for the required sacrifice.[4]

The Igbo community would make an *Mbari*[5] and leave it as a sacrifice, not just of property but of time, skills and community effort. There are also legends and sagas telling us of how in dire circumstances human beings have been sacrificed to restore health, wholeness and safety to whole communities. Whether it is to cleanse or to pre-empt, the net expectation is that sacrifice will result in harmony and fullness of life.

In giving up non-human things, what is given up has no will of its own; yet the sacrifice is, or is expected to be, efficacious, because it represents the willingness of the human-offerers to "give up" what they see as their possession in order to bring about more good. What matters is that, given the choice, they have picked an alternative which they believe to be the will of God. The practice of sacrifice then represents the recognition of one's sinfulness and the willingness to seek and accept the forgiveness of God which we receive upon leaving our own way to follow God's. The ritual practices are the outward signs of our giving up our false pride and

---

[4] S.N. Ezeanya, "Women in African Traditional Religion"; *Ibadan Journal of Religious Studies*. Vol. X/2 Dec. 1976, pp.109-110.

[5] J.O. Okparocha, *Mbari: Art as Sacrifice*, Ibadan, Daystar Press, 1977. Moremi is the heroine of a legend emanating from Ife, the centre of Yoruba people. She by a promise to sacrifice her son to the River Osimari was given to discover the secrets of the Igbo people who by subterfuge conducted an annual raid on the Ife. When the Ife had unmasked the Igbo and driven them away, Moremi like Jephtah sacrificed the young man in fulfilment of her vow.

inordinate self-esteem. In the sacrifice of thanksgiving, which in Africa often involves feeding all and sundry and in distributing gifts, one sees the affirmation that sharing and communion are necessary components of life in community. In African traditional society one is truly a person only as one is able to lay claim to "belonging", and to belong is to faithfully serve the group welfare and to desist from whatever is deemed to bring *mmusu* (all that is anti-life) into the community, for both your triumphs and failures belong not only to you personally but to the whole group. Hence the apparent acquiescence of many women in situations that as *individuals* they would not accept.

In the socio-cultural ethos of traditional Africa, women are deemed to be living truly feminine lives as they give up what they could have been and conform to the community's image of womanhood, which is built upon the survival, physically, of the human race. One has only to read the obituaries of women in Nigerian dailies to get an idea of the model of womanhood in the society.[6] Among the matrilineal Akan of Ghana, "mother" is the foundation of the community. To stamp this firmly on the psyche of every member is the saying *Nsamanpow mu soduro, wo ni wu a w'abusua asa* which, interpreted broadly, makes the assertion that the demise of the mother is the demise of the family unit. None disputes this notion that the woman is the glue that holds society together. But what sort of a society and what sort of glue? Is she simply a catalyst that makes things work without herself being changed, "an agent of societal stability" who herself remains stable, oblivious of the changes around her? These are not rhetorical questions for they embody some of the very crucial debates as to who the woman is or should be. Onibukun says:

> In our society, it appears as if women make more sacrifice for societal cohesion by working hard at marital stability. Married women make living comfortable and enjoyable for their husbands by being the men's cook, home keeper, mother of his children, laundry person, friend, playmate, counsellor etc. Women sacrifice their careers and ambition for the furtherance of those of the men; simply put, "women help the men to progress".[7]

---

[6] Several if not most refer to their *wifely and or motherly* duties, describing them as being devoted, loving and dutiful. Below was what was said about one described as grand-mother and great-grand-mother. "Our dutiful and beloved ... who answered her creator's call a year ago... a loving mother and devoted Christian your life is a shining example... the qualities of your being a good mother etc. and wife are seen by us every day even after your death..." Or again this said of a 53 year-old: "Like a beautiful castle you collapsed, exposing us to the bitter and harsh weather of this wicked world."

[7] O.M. Onibukun, "Women as Agent of Societal Stability", paper presented at the 8th Biennial Conference of the Nigerian Association of University Woman, 4-7 November 1982, p.5.

Onibukun affirms that women perform humanitarian services that are "very essential for maintaining the status quo"; they sacrifice time and money for the handicapped and the aged; they even get a mention for providing "societal needs that are not publicly recognized" by submitting themselves to prostitution, thus forestalling the "unpalatable" outcome of unmet strains.[8]

The author seems to feel quite comfortable with this situation for in her conclusion she states:

> If more women are educated, they will be able to apply their knowledge to improve the quality of service rendered to their husbands, children and their society.[9]

I have made such extensive reference to this paper because it underlines the general acceptance of the sacrificial role of women in Africa. I have nothing against living for others but I question intensely the quality and style of life demanded as well as the standards by which we measure "the life that is life indeed", when dealing with women.

Take one of the reasons why women exult in marriage and have set themselves up as the promoters and defenders of the institution and its ambiguous practices and norms. For the sake of the children, we say. A very noble, self-abnegating principle, but what exactly does the bad marriage do to the souls of the children born of it? Is it really for the sake of the children, or for the pride that refuses to admit failure, or for fear of the insecurity outside marriage? What is to be sacrificed to a bad marriage — the personality and attitudes of the growing children or the pride of the woman? On the other hand, as we have seen, there is no doubt that when a woman curtails public life and professional advancement for the sake of husband and children and home, and, as often happens, even "loses her personal identity", she is making a worthy sacrifice. She is giving up the most precious gift she has, "her life", that others might live more fully. In some of these situations she is making a sacrifice, but in others she is really being sacrificed.

Growing up in the Methodist manses of Ghana I became familiar with the phrase "the pillars of the church", referring to women who give themselves up to the work of the church, strong posts that almost literally hold up the roofs of chapels — with money and physical strength as well as with the power and silence of a column in a cathedral. When they

---

[8] *Ibid.*, p.7.
[9] *Ibid.*

speak, the whole fabric of the church quakes with what I see as an unnecessary fear: the fear that the status quo will be upset, fear that the magnificent edifices of suppression will collapse, and a faithless fear that when it does a more appropriate structure cannot emerge. Allowing such fears to paralyze the church is for me a declaration that human sin is bound to prevail against the will of God, a statement no Christian will subscribe to but to which many bow by the lives they live.

Hence in church, as in society, "women's role" as custodians of stability does involve *refrain*, both in the sense of repeating what has been and that of keeping away from being bearers of *the new*.   The foregoing does not come from historical or anthropological studies, nor does it apply only to rural sectors of the continent but to all women in all walks of life in today's Africa. All women are expected to deny themselves that others may have more space in which to develop. Women are expected to drop all to accompany husbands who go abroad to study, and therefore scholarships to men include facilities for the spouse to accompany, not so much for the women themselves. The assumption is that *her presence* will facilitate *his studies* whereas no thought is given to the possibility that *his presence* might facilitate *her studies*. The principle here seems to be that whereas *the woman completes the man, the woman is deemed complete by herself*, the exception being made when her dependence on her spouse is to the advantage of the institutions. In both cases she is the "sacrificial lamb". Her career and self-esteem are promoted only to the extent that it is beneficial to "the other". For few are the institutions which assume that a husband might need to or even want to accompany his wife. All talk of keeping families together is founded on the domiciliary arrangement whereby the man "provides" for the woman and she responds by serving his interests in the hope that some of his interests will coincide with hers.

Thus in one way or another self-denial becomes the way of life for a woman. She lives a sort of permanent "kenosis" as a condition that is demanded of her, not in the manner of Christ, undertaken voluntarily, for "he did not count equality with God a thing to be grasped, but emptied himself, taking the form of a servant" (Phil. 2:6-7).

It seems to me that the "expected kenosis" of women and their compliance have enabled men to be the chief architects of history. For good or ill women stabilize the situations men create. I do not therefore entertain any romantic notions about sacrifice. I am pointing to sacrifice only in so far as it promotes the values and life-style of the kingdom of God, and in so far as it is enjoined on both churchwomen and churchmen alike.

Whether it is self-sacrifice or a case of "being sacrificed", the level and mode of participation of women in church and society is a demonstration of the necessity for sacrifice in order to be in mission.

The church has stressed the sociological assertion of the humanity and the *raison d'etre* of the woman for its "survival". This was what Paul required of the women of Corinth. So much so that when the church is confronted with evidence of women "bearing rule" in the ancient church, it is set aside as abnormal. When contemporary experience demonstrates the indefensibility of relegating women to the sidelines, the church declares it is not obliged to follow society's dictates. Faced with such intransigence and the constant presentation of tradition as norm, some women have come to the conclusion that they will lay aside any call to the representative ministry and not seek ordination so as not to be a *skandalon* to the "weaker brethren". They do so in the same spirit as the women who refrain from developing aspects of their personalities and innate abilities for the sake of the family or in accordance with the dictates of the traditions and mores of society.

Emptying the church

If the woman's sacrifice is as deliberate as here described, it is a "reasonable sacrifice" in the sense that it is reasoned. It is this deliberate sacrifice that I wish to present as a process of "self-emptying".

In recent years some African women have answered the call to the representative ministry, sought and obtained their church's recognition of their call, and are serving under the "order" and discipline of these churches. As persons these women may or may not effect any appreciable changes in our traditional understanding of authority in relation to the representative ministry and may make no sacrifice — except run the risk of being seen as freaks, carrying with them the disabilities imposed by an unreformed community that fails to accept the personhood of the woman as "being in the image of God".

Most important, however, are the hosts of unsung women and men — non-stipendiaries — who carry on the mission of the church, but whose place in ecclesiological treatises is usually reduced to a sentence or at most a paragraph on the "priesthood of all believers", a statement whose consequences we often prefer to leave unexamined.

As a substantial sector of the laity, women give, without counting the cost and often without the privilege of determining what the church ought to be about. The church has become for churchwomen a third altar on which they sacrifice or are sacrificed. But this paper is not about the merits or demerits, theological or otherwise, of this way of perceiving and ordering womanhood. It poses the question whether the church's mission would not be better promoted, enhanced and executed if *all*, not just women, learn to operate in the spirit of *self*-denial. My position is that the church can begin to function more effectively as an instrument of Christ if it models itself on the sacrificial life of the woman, indeed of Christ himself. Socialized to love, the woman holds together the fabric of society by her costly giving of herself. This living for the other, yes, dying for "friends" is the ultimate evidence of "greater love" which in the final analysis is the only agent of history that struggles to conform to God's project of a new humanity in a new society and to the culminating purpose of making all things new.

Jesus, who is the foundation of the church's mission, leaves us with no illusions about the difficulties inherent in the demands of God whose kingdom the church's mission seeks to foster. His own salvific mission was undertaken in the context of constant submission to the will of God, voluntarily adhered to as in the original "laying aside" of his divinity enshrined for us in the hymn found in the letter to the Philippians cited above.

What will such a self-emptying mean for the church? My observation tends to indicate that whereas the church affirms the death and resurrection of Christ as an indication of the power of powerlessness, in Africa at any rate, it tries to hold on to power; and that in spite of the dominical dictum that to gain true life we must be prepared to lose our life for his sake, the church and its institutions in Africa are trying desperately to hold on to power as a means of holding on to life. In places where the church was represented by a denomination that is in tune with the colonial power (e.g. Anglicans in the British colonies, Roman Catholics in Spanish and Portuguese colonies) it is often assumed that some ground is lost when state occasions do not have a specifically Christian colour. I hear Christians speak with a note of alarm about the Legal Year religious service being held in a mosque rather than in a church. Prestige is at stake. There is similar panic built around government take-over of private institutions (hospitals and schools) which sap so much energy that little creative thinking has gone into making effective the church's mandate to heal and to teach. Here the woman as a model becomes apposite. Faced with a life of service to others women have constantly created alternative life-styles, fully convinced that in serving others their lives are enriched.

When serving has meant mothering and home-making at an early age, women have so ordered their lives that at 40 they come to university degrees with their teenage daughter or son graduating at the same ceremony. Some do the same at second degrees to the delight of the whole family.

Women confined to home and hearth during traditional festivals spend the time happily preparing the delicacies which the ordinary routine of life prevents them from making. In the event a joyful feast is laid for all, but more important, feeding the hungry is transformed from a chore to a work of art.

Women deprived of male support in time of war, by immigration or death, have proved that history-making does not belong to men alone and hence blazed new avenues — later to be labelled "women's role" — until men find it convenient to join in (e.g. nursing and secretarial skills).

Women who feel "sacrificed" for no just and honourable cause have protested and called for dialogue to reason out the situation.

Women do all this because, created to be fully and truly human, they have in them the ability not only to adapt for the purpose of survival but to be creative as beings linked with the Creator-God. Several women who have thought out their *raison d'etre* have come to the conclusion that the survival of a healthy society depends upon their sacrificial lives. Thus they take the position of the young Mary who submitted herself to the will of God and so became *theotokos*, the bearer of God. A Christ-bearing church will have to empty itself of all pride, self-seeking and, above all, of the fear of death, not to talk of pomp and circumstances surrounding its participation on state occasions. The churches must be like the young girl who braved the ignominy of bearing an "illegitimate child" and, I imagine, the loss of a "society wedding" she had been dreaming of during all her maiden days, assured only by the words of an angel that she was in the employ of God.

The church's charge

When the church adopts a posture of sacrificing, it will not be doing so only for the sake of mission; it will find herself actually in mission. In Africa, where several countries are beginning to show wide gaps between those who enjoy material wellbeing and those who are simply surviving, churches are found hoarding God's gifts. Land, money, property lie unused or partially utilized. Land that could be farmed or turned into sites for social amenities, buildings that are used only a few hours a day, when even Christian education goes unattended to, money that goes into importing pipe organs when youth programmes become shallower and shallower — sacrificing these will move Christians closer to the "living sacrifice" they claim to be.

In the socio-economic and political situation of Africa the poor and lowly easily become victims of the upheavals associated with instability and economic chaos. The church in mission has a message of good news to the poor, the oppressed, the shackled, and the physically and spiritually handicapped. How is this message to be delivered? Some risk-taking is involved in taking up advocacy for the poor, the disinherited and the voiceless. Albert van den Heuvel, a former director of the Youth Department of the World Council of Churches, speaking to a conference of the Student Christian Movement in the 1960s, had the following to say about what he called the "humiliation of the church":

> The humiliation of the church is her *raison d'etre*... the real humiliation is that we refuse to be humiliated. Imagine what would happen if the church really listened to the New Testament description and lived up to her [reason for] existence of being bought and put to work like a slave girl of mankind. That is the challenge we have to live up to.

To be a "slave girl of mankind" the church in Africa will have to sacrifice security and risk calumny if not persecution. If it undertakes to work against the negative effects of multinationals and transnationals (including world confessional families), it will be taken to task by those who hold the reigns of control and those who are controlled by the system. These global organizations, supposedly international, exhibit traits that can be properly described as imperialistic, for what they do is to build "empires", spheres of influence within which the will of those who have the power prevails. Perhaps some churches in Africa need to sacrifice the comfort and security of their "confessional families" for more authenticity and relevance at home, for those who undertake to proclaim the kingdom and to baptize in the Name must carry conviction that in the place where they are, the Gospel can become "power unto salvation".

Being sacrificed

Following our paradigm of the lives of women, we observe that in society as in the church there are women who are sacrificed in order that things may remain as they are. The reluctance of some churches to consider the ordination of women into the representative ministry (episcopate, presbyterate and diaconate) does in this analysis fall into the category of "women being sacrificed".

Since this means that one's charisma, including the gift of ordination into the representative ministries, may only operate within the juridical system, bishops and conferences have successfully denied women the opportunity to obey the call of the Holy Spirit. The question arises as to whether this is simply a devise to enhance the male ego through the deification of existing structures or the refusal to re-examine tradition for fear its foundations cannot stand?

And women are sacrificed on the altar of unity. It is clear that the Christian community unable to achieve visible unity, for various reasons, has decided to sacrifice the call of women, alleging that the issues involved in unity conversations will be further compounded and complicated by the ordination of women into the representative ministry of some of the partners in the conversations. An Irish Roman Catholic nun had this to say: "If the Anglicans were really convinced of the validity of women's ministries they would have challenged the Orthodox and Catholic view rather than simply deferring to it." I share her evaluation of the situation. Women have once again been sacrificed.

For me the impasse has arisen out of the associations of authority with the ordained ministry. Ordination is interpreted as "bearing rule" or "having authority" and it is culturally inconceivable to envisage women in that role. Yet, should the church view the factor of "authority" from the lives of women it will discover that for women *exousia* carries prominently a content of *responsibility*. The responsibilities given to women in church and society are executed with the authority of love, which operates in antithesis to the male concept of *exousia* as autocracy. If the *exousia* of the people under orders in the church could be transformed by this perspective, the mission of the church could become more effective.

My thesis, then, is that if the church can begin to function more effectively as an instrument of Christ it must follow the sacrificial life of the woman. Not as the sacrificed, but as the one consciously and deliberately becoming a living sacrifice, taking up the cross voluntarily. In this way it will be following its Lord who dedicated his whole life to the announcement of the kingdom by word and deed.

What I see, however, is a church being led to the altar of conformity by Christians themselves, through socio-political pressures and denominational loyalties. It looks to me like a sacrificial lamb, not a living sacrifice. It is not a martyr because there is no bold confession of faith in particular situations, only acquiescence. The consequence is the virtual ineffectiveness of the church in Africa. It is taken for granted, for it has allowed itself to be silenced. In such a situation it loses its prophetic mission and tamely undertakes to condone or back un-Christian courses — racism in South Africa, ethnic hostility and discrimination, blatant neglect of rural areas, irrelevance in the search for appropriate education and the creation of work experience and job opportunity — while in some countries it joins in the chorus of praising governments that do not deserve such praise. Even when it has spoken what seems to be the word in season, it is suspected to be doing so out of bourgeois considerations because of its seemingly comfortable posture. Its tirade against bribery and corruption, against moral laxity and nepotism goes unheeded in Africa; it has become a question of "see who's talking".

We have looked at the mission of the church from the perspective of sacrifice, focusing specifically on the lives of women in Africa. We have called attention to the experience of churchwomen, which is not just African but is similar in many parts of the world and of the church. We have also attempted to make a distinction between making a sacrifice and being sacrificed, enjoining the church and individual Christians to live according to the former and to eschew the latter, a position demanded of them as people whose salvation and mission derive from the self-emptying of Jesus Christ. In the process we demonstrate our solidarity with the world for which Christ died and for which we give thanks in the eucharist, the constant anamnesis of his sacrifice.

In our world people no longer accept material poverty as destined or as the result of laziness. In Africa today people are prepared to die for their humanity and even for that of others. The church's solidarity with such a world will only become evident as it becomes a place where the poor, the voiceless and powerless will be given a voice and empowered to combat all the forces of dehumanization. The church has a mandate to seek the kingdom of God and its righteousness, righteousness understood not only in the Pauline sense of justification by the grace of God but also in the sense of right relationship between persons and above all in our relating to God. In that way right-doing and right-living will become embedded in the church and not simply emanate as words from our pulpits.

When we are ready to sacrifice the pomp and circumstance and security and to put on humility, being gentle as doves and wise and serpents, we shall be a church that is truly in mission.

III. Mission of Women in the Church in Asia: Role and Position

Virginia Fabella

I am looking at an Asian woman:

"She has a round face," but it is hidden behind a veil.

"She has curved eyes" which are shut in the daytime as she entertains men all night.

"She has a small nose" which has got used to the stench of the slums and the pollution of the city.

"She has short legs" — or are they simply an "elephant's hind legs".

"She is short in height" — and getting bent because of the double or triple oppression she bears.

"She is elegant and graceful" but no one notices since she's busy all day taking orders — from men.[1]

Do you recognize her? You may say she is the oppressed woman in Asia. But isn't the oppressed woman also our sister? Isn't she also ourselves?

I believe that all Christians have the same basic mission, whether they be lay, cleric or religious, whether they be male or female — and that is to continue the mission of Jesus Christ on earth. The mission of Jesus is summarized succinctly in John 10:10: "I have come that all may have life and have it to the full." This is God's plan for all humanity, which St Ireneus expressed in his famous phrase: "The glory of God is the human being fully alive."

We have the double obligation to take this mission earnestly, especially in Asia, where the diminishment of life is evidenced by the poverty, oppression, misery and the lack of fulfilment of the majority of our

---

[1] The description is quoted from the introduction of Sister Kim Ok Hy's talk, "Women in the History of Catholicism in Korea," given at the Seventh Asian Meeting of Religious. The phrase "elephant's hind legs" is from an old Thai saying quoted in the Thailand country report for AMOR VII: "Men are the forelegs of an elephant; women are the hind legs."

people. Together with all who take their Christianity seriously, we have the self-same mission to help our Asian brothers and sisters attain the life in abundance that Jesus came to bring.

My reflections on women in the church will be divided into two sections: the first on women in the church as *disciples*, and the second, on women in the church as *women*.

This first section will have three parts: Mary as model of discipleship; the disciples as equals in the early church; Christian disciples in Asia. The second section will have three corresponding parts: Mary as model of womanhood; the distinction between equality and complementarity; women in inculturation and liberation.

So first, as *disciples*. As discipleship is not limited to women, the reflections under this section are actually applicable to both men and women in the church. In general terms, a disciple is one who accepts and promotes the teachings of another. The Gospel writers are in agreement that a true disciple of Jesus is one who hears the word of God and acts upon it. For St Luke, the first and exemplary disciple is Mary, the mother of Jesus. Luke portrays Mary as a young maiden who accepts the challenge of the Holy Spirit at the Annunciation, as one who ponders God's word in her heart and responds with courage and determination, as one who is ever ready to be of service to her neighbour, as one who, while persevering in prayer, is filled with the Spirit of prophecy and justice together with the other disciples at Pentecost.

For too long, Mary has been depicted for us principally as "virgin" and "mother" — rarely as "disciple". Yet for Jesus himself, physical motherhood, important as it is, is not the basis of his own mother's greatness. For Jesus, discipleship has priority over family ties. Pointing to his disciples, he said: "Here are my mother and my brothers. For whoever does the will of my Father in heaven is my brother and sister and mother" (Matt. 12:49-50). Mary's special claim is not her having given birth to Jesus, but that she qualified and formed part of Jesus' family of disciples through her obedient response to God's word. Mary then remains a model for all Christians, not so much of motherhood as of faith and discipleship.

The community of disciples Jesus brought into existence definitely included a number of women. We gather this even from the sparse references to women in the New Testament. Given the male-oriented and androcentric bias of the New Testament authors, we can deduce that what is available to us in scriptures is only a fraction of the information which was available to the writers then. What was de-emphasized by the writers is the fact that women were part of the discipleship of equals that existed for a period in early Christianity. A non-androcentric reconstruction of early church history reveals that during the early church, women were full-fledged disciples, and equally missionaries, prophets, church leaders, and apostles in the broad sense of the term.

As Elisabeth Fiorenza, noted author and New Testament scholar, observes:

> The new self-understanding of the Christians did away with all religious, class, social and patriarchal relationships of dominance, and therefore made it possible not only for Gentiles and slaves, but also for women to assume leadership functions within the urban missionary movement. In this movement, women were not marginal figures but exercised leadership as missionaries, founders of Christian communities, apostles, prophets and leaders of churches.[2]

For example, Junia, together with her husband Andronicus, was an influential missionary who was acknowledged as an apostle, even before Paul (Rom. 16:7).[3] Phoebe was Paul's co-worker, most likely an official minister and teacher in the church in Cenchreae, whose authority was respected even by Paul himself (Rom. 16:1-3). Nympha was a founder and leader of a house church in Laodicea (Col. 4:15). These few examples from Paul's letters give us a glimpse of the egalitarian church that was alive in early Christianity but which fell victim to the progressive patriarchalization and institutionalization of the church as it took over the patriarchal, institutional structures of Greco-Roman society.

Some claim that this progressive patriarchalization of the church in its interpretation and action was unavoidable and is now irreversible. All disciples who have become aware of this recent research on early church tradition and practice have the special responsibility to challenge this claim. How can we as disciples who seek a full life for all be content with a relationship of inequality and dominance within the very church committed to God's kingdom and God's justice? Clearly there must be a concerted effort to recapture the early egalitarian model of *ecclesia*, which was based on the equality of all Christians, male and female alike.

The recent phenomenon of basic ecclesial communities or BECs is

---

[2] "'You Are Not to Be Called Father': Early Christian History in a Feminist Perspective", in *The Bible and Liberation*, ed. Norman K. Gottwald, Maryknoll, N.Y., Orbis Books, 1983, p.411.

[3] Cf. Elisabeth Schussler Fiorenza, "Women in the Pre-Pauline and Pauline Churches", *Union Seminary Quarterly Review*, Vol. 33, Nos 3 and 4, Spring and Summer 1978, especially pp.155-158.

closer to this egalitarian model of *ecclesia* than the hierarchical model still persisting in the universal church today; therefore BECs should be encouraged especially in rural and depressed areas and become the locus of new and creative ministries for both men and women in the church today.

So far we have looked at discipleship in relation to church and our faith. But equally important is to look at discipleship within the context of the vast continent of Asia. Asia is the most varied and complex of all the continents, yet a sweeping overview reveals that it has two glaring characteristics: massive poverty and oppression on the one hand and the rich diversity of cultures and religious traditions on the other. We need to address these two facets of our reality if we are to be a relevant presence in the Asian context, if we are to give meaningful responses to our people's claim to a fully human existence, if we are to express our faith and faith reflections in a manner that is truly Asian.

The challenges of our Asian reality have evoked two main responses on the part of church people:
1) the promotion of justice and participation in social transformation in response to the massive poverty and oppression; and
2) the inculturation of the faith, coupled with inter-religious dialogue, in response to the multi-faceted religiosity.

When the Asian bishops assembled in 1974 to reflect on "Evangelization in Modern Day Asia", they recognized the need for both.[4] When they proclaimed that the focus of evangelization in Asia should be on the building of truly local churches, they saw that in order to have a truly local church, it has to be inculturated and indigenized, in dialogue with the local cultures, religions and living traditions, sinking its roots in the people's life and history, and seeking to share in whatever truly belongs to the people: their thoughts, meanings, values, aspirations. At the same time, the bishops recognized that a truly local church in Asia must necessarily be in dialogue with the poor, for most of Asia is made up of multitudes of the poor and marginalized groups who live under oppression and are deprived of access to opportunities and material resources needed to create a truly human life for themselves. This is what the bishops termed "a dialogue of life" — a dialogue with the poor, which involves working not so much *for* them as *with* them, learning from them

---

[4] Cf. *Evangelization in Modern Day Asia*, Statement of the First Plenary Assembly of the Federation of Asian Bishops' Conferences, Taipei, Taiwan, 22-27 April 1974, 3rd revised edition, especially Sections 9-24.

and striving together with them to transform those structures and situations which keep them in that deprivation and powerlessness.

Thus both the inculturation of the faith, which includes inter-religious dialogue, and liberation from unjust social structures are necessary and urgent tasks in Asia. Unfortunately, instead of being seen as twin facets of evangelization, they are oftentimes taken as unrelated tasks, or worse, in opposition to each other. At times there is mutual suspicion between workers in these two areas: the "inculturationists" see the work of the "liberationists" as pure political activism divorced from the gospel, while the "liberationists" see the work of "inculturationists" as irrelevant in a continent crying out for justice and human rights.

But we have the example of the incarnation. The Son of God not only took on human form but immersed himself in the total life and culture of the Jewish people. It was only in so doing that he could be the liberating Lord of the gospel, who could speak knowledgeably and act with confidence to free men and women from the oppressive religious and societal customs and situations of his day. Following the principle of incarnation, it would be a mistake to keep the two tasks of inculturation and liberation separate. Michael Amaladoss, an Indian Jesuit, sees them as closely related. In speaking on "inculturation" before superiors general in Rome, he said that today we need a broadened and deepened understanding of inculturation to signify "the process of building up a new humanity embracing... the proclamation of the Good News, dialogue, action for liberation, and community-building..."[5]

In fact, both inculturation and liberation have a commonality in their effort towards freedom from external domination, pressure, or undue influences. Part of the task of liberation is disengagement from foreign control, principally political and economic, but also cultural. Part of the task of inculturation is discerning whether some aspects of the faith being rooted in the native soil may be nothing but Western culture cloaked as the gospel, or whether some of the religious practices Asians have adopted may not be more *Roman* than *Catholic*.

Amaladoss in the same talk on "inculturation" cautions that if the goal of inculturation is ultimately the building of a new human community, then it is the task not of a few experts (and here we can translate: a few religious men and women), but of the people. Similarly, true liberation can be achieved only if it emerges from the people's own struggle, not that of a few elite.

---

[5] "Inculturation," *SEDOS Bulletin*, 84/No. 13, 15 September 1984, p.304.

In Asia, then, it is only when we have integrated the work of inculturation and liberation that we can hope for the church's truly meaningful presence in the continent. It is only then that we can speak of authentically local churches with a spirituality and a theology that are truly Asian.

In the light of what has been said, one wonders if there is any responsibility that remains exclusively ours as women in the church in Asia. Actually I don't believe there is any line of service or function in the church that should be the exclusive responsibility of either men or women. However, given the present reality of a church that is still heavily laden with patriarchal structures and practices, church women have to assume certain responsibilities for themselves until such time when they, together with all other women, can take their rightful place in the church and in society.

We have remarked in the first section that for centuries, Mary has been portrayed principally as "virgin" and "mother". There was little stress on Mary as disciple until recently. Likewise there has been little stress on Mary as woman until very recently. Yet Jesus himself had great esteem for his own mother as *woman*. In St John's Gospel, Mary is shown as being present at the beginning and at the end of Jesus' public ministry — at the wedding feast in Cana and at the foot of the cross. In both instances, Jesus addressed his mother not as "mother" but as "woman". Recently, some biblical scholars, both Catholic and Protestant, published a book on Mary[6] where they note that the title "woman" is not a common or known way of addressing one's mother in the Israel of Jesus' time. Jesus also uses the term to address other women; however, it cannot be concluded that this is Jesus' way of addressing women in general for, in speaking to Mary of Magdala after the resurrection, he calls her "woman" but also by name. Neither can it be concluded that this was a derogatory form of address for Jesus, as he is never shown as having a negative attitude towards women or treating them in a demeaning or condescending manner, while he is known to have criticized sharply the religious authorities, all male, and even Peter. One can only conclude that "woman" is a respectful term of address for Jesus; and when he uses it in speaking to his mother, he is affirming that he not only values her womanhood, but that being woman had priority over being mother in the new dispensation.

---

6 Raymond E. Brown *et al.*, eds, *Mary in the New Testament*, Quezon City, Claretian Publications, 1984, pp. 188-189.

However, such has not been the high value accorded to womanhood through the past centuries, not even within Christianity. History shows that religion has been used to perpetuate the inferior position of women, and it is known that all major religions are still guilty of discriminating against women in varying degrees today. Sad to say, the Christian Church is no exception.

One of the ways Catholicism, for example, has contributed to the subordination of women, especially in the church, is by its portrayal of Mary through the ages. Mary has been depicted as silent, sweet, self-effacing, docile, passive, submissive, a Mater Dolorosa. Actually this portrayal of Mary is a masculine perception of idealized femininity which has been inflicted on us and which many of us in turn have tried hard to internalize. In recent times, however, women have begun to appropriate the Bible for themselves without the mediation of male interpreters, and realize how Mary has been misrepresented. They see Mary of the Gospels, especially of the Magnificat, as a woman of faith and intelligence, who is gentle and attentive, yet decisive and responsive, a woman of deep compassion but also of great courage, who is able to take initiatives and make great sacrifices, and is willing to risk in order to accomplish God's word and will. This is to a growing number of women — and should be to us — the true Mary, who is proto-disciple, yes, but above all, *woman*.

As women in the church, isn't it our responsibility to foster a reportrayal of Mary that is closer to the gospel, as women scripture scholars are uncovering? To allow a continued distortion of Mary's image is in fact to perpetuate a characterization of womanhood that is both restricting and deforming, if not dehumanizing.

If Mary's image has undergone a distortion, doesn't this lead us to suspect that there might be other distortions in other parts of the gospel, when interpreted exclusively by male exegetes? There is need for a re-reading of the Bible from women's perspectives so that both men and women alike can enjoy its liberating message. I hope that religious congregations in Asia will start releasing some of their members for serious biblical studies that could contribute to a more inclusive interpretation of the scriptures — for there is need for a re-reading of God's message not only from the perspective of women but of Asia as well. For too long, the interpretation of scriptures has been the monopoly of the male and the West.

In the first section, we spoke of the discipleship of equals in the early church. No one is saying that there is no distinction between the sexes, rather, that both are equally human, made in God's image. Both are ordained to subdue the earth and rule over the rest of creation, not one over the other.

It is then not a question of whether women want to be equal with men. It is simply the way God, as just and loving Creator, willed to create men and women. Jesus meant full life for all, not only for half the human race.

Care must be taken that complementarity is not confused with equality. We recall from mathematics, especially from our geometry classes, that angles are complementary if together they make up 90 degrees. It doesn't matter if one is 80 degrees and the other 10. When people insist that men and women should play complementary roles or perform complementary functions in the church we have to make sure they do not mean that men take the leadership roles and functions, while women assume the subsidiary ones, that men make the decisions and women implement them. The complementarity that respects equality means both men and women should share in decision-making in matters that affect them both, just as both should share in the exercise of "spiritual motherhood" since both are called to care for their neighbour so that their neighbour may have life to the full. If there are differences in the role and functions, they should be based on charism and capability, not on gender. As long as men dominate the church, church women have the added responsibility to make people aware of this discrepancy between equality and complementarity when people insist on complementarity. Complementarity is acceptable only if it respects equality.

Finally, we spoke of the twin tasks of inculturation and liberation needed in Asia today. Inculturation is deeper than mere adaptation. It is often referred to as the dialogue between gospel and culture. But we must be careful that in our zeal for inculturation we do not destroy our ability to criticize culture. There are aspects of cultures and religions which have been oppressive and even dehumanizing, especially for women. Women in the church involved in inculturation have to see to it that this important work, which is a long-term process, is accompanied by a serious analysis of the local culture and religion to detect which aspects or developments of the culture and religion are life-giving and liberating and which are domesticating and alienating. This analysis of religion should be assiduously applied even to our own. In fact, a comprehensive analysis of the socio-political, economic, cultural and religious realities should be part and parcel of the work of both inculturation and liberation.

Women in the church also have some serious responsibilities in the work for justice and liberation. The people in Asia who suffer the greatest are the women; they are the most exploited and deprived, the most vulnerable and powerless. Recently, however, women of the different labour sectors have started to awaken, to protest their degradation and the violation of their rights, and to struggle for integral liberation. As women in the church, we cannot dissociate ourselves from women's movements for justice, equality and liberation, if we really desire to see all women treated as equals in society. We need to question ourselves if we find ourselves hesitating to offer more than our prayers, if we find ourselves refusing to join them in their demands for equal opportunities and a more human life. As women in the church, we need to explore new ministries with and on behalf of women who need our support, our defence, our presence, our solidarity, our friendship. And in Asia they are countless.

As women religious, are we willing to risk criticism and venture into new apostolates to help our less privileged sisters on the farm, in the factory, in the kitchen, or will we find excuses when they appeal to us for help, and say that it is not within our congregational charism? Once Jesus said to the Pharisees and teachers of the Law: "You have a fine way of setting aside the commands of God in order to observe your own traditions" (Mark 7:8).

The aim of women's liberation and struggle for equality in the church and in society is not to get even with men or to replace them as oppressors. The true end of our struggles is a more just and human society for all, a society that reflects God's kingdom of love, truth, justice and peace. But liberation will come only if we first admit we need it, only if we truly want it, only if we are willing to struggle for it with all the other women — together.

Once again I am looking at an Asian woman:

> She has a round face, a small nose.
> She has short legs.
> She is short in height.
> She is elegant and graceful.

She hears a voice assuring her: Woman, you are set free from your infirmities (Luke 13:12). And immediately she stands up and praises God.

IV. God Weeps with Our Pain

Kwok Pui Lan

You ask me what shape feminist theology in Asia will take. Will it start with "beyond God the Father"[1] and finish with "beginning from the other end"?[2] Will it be coloured by the rhetoric of middle-class elites or heavily laden with socialist terminology? Will it yield a systematic analysis of the situation of women in Asia or just an emotional outburst like that of a lunatic?

For these questions, I have no answer. I only know that feminist theology in Asia will be a cry, a plea and an invocation. It emerges from the wounds that hurt, the scars that do not disappear, the stories that have no ending. Feminist theology in Asia is not written with a pen, it is inscribed on the hearts of many who feel the pain, and yet dare to hope.

Suffering of the no-body

I would like to tell you a story, a story that makes people cry.

Ah Ching is a little girl who lives in a village in China. Her parents are hard-working peasants. Ah Ching's father likes the little girl but he wants to have a son. One night when Ah Ching was asleep, she suddenly felt a heavy blanket being pulled over her and she could hardly breathe. She struggled and yelled: "Mama, Mama, help, help me!" To her amazement, she found that the one who tried to suffocate her was her father! She cried and prayed that her father would let her go and she promised to be a good girl.

---

[1] Mary Daly criticized the patriarchal terminology and images of the Judeo-Christian tradition. See her *Beyond God the Father*, Boston, Beacon Press, 1973.

[2] Letty Russell often said we should begin from the other end, from the new creation rather than from the old. Refer to Letty Russell, "Theological Aspects of the Partnership of Women and Men in Christian Communities", *Pro Mundi Vita Bulletin*, No. 59, March 1976, pp.4-10.

Ah Ching was so afraid that when dawn broke she escaped from the farm house and went to seek refuge with her old grandma.

When the grandma heard the story, she was so sad that tears began to run down her wrinkled cheeks. The night came, and grandma put Ah Ching to bed and comforted her. But at midnight, grandma, summoning all her strength, with her trembling hands suffocated Ah Ching with an old blanket...[3]

China, over-burdened with her one billion population, is determined to maintain a low birth-rate. A strict population control policy is implemented and couples are persuaded or coerced by various measures to have one child only. In the past, giving birth to a girl was regarded as bad luck, but now having a girl means an end to the family's future. Ah Ching's mother prayed day and night for a boy and she wept bitterly when Ah Ching was born. These tears were cried for Ah Ching, for herself, for her family, and for the thousands of years of patriarchal tradition that still haunt people's minds after thirty years of socialist reconstruction and after the so-called Cultural Revolution! Many women in China and in Asia on similar occasions must have wept too. Sarah and Hannah back in the old days had also cried out to their God.

Women are the poorest among the poor, the most voiceless among the oppressed, the most exploited. Sister Mary John Mananzan, in her study of sexual exploitation in a third world setting, lamented: "In an underdeveloped, exploited country, women tend to bear the burden of a double exploitation because of their sex."[4] In the so-called "legalized prostitution area" in Jakarta, eight to ten girls live in one house. Behind the dining room, they have separate little compartments for doing their business. Each girl has her nice-looking photograph with her name on a board in the dining room. The customer comes in, looks at the photographs, picks one from them as if choosing something from the menu. Some of the girls in Thailand and in the Philippines have no names, they only wear a number.

If you walk down the red-light district in Taipei, you can see those women sitting by the window. Their heavy make-up cannot conceal their pale faces and grotesque eyes. When business is poor, the "mother" will come on to the street and offer the woman to the Hong Kong tourist passers-by in her awkward Cantonese. The vulgar Cantonese slang not

---

[3] A story I heard personally from a journalist.
[4] "Sexual Exploitation in a Third World Setting", in *Women in Asia: Status and Image*, Singapore, Christian Conference of Asia, 1979, p.25.

only embarrasses those who hear it but forces one to understand what "sex object" means. Those women are no longer treated as human beings with a body, they are literally "no-body".

Sexual exploitation does not only ruin a woman's body and soul, it rapes the land too. As Sister Mary John so forcefully points out, prostitution has so much to do with sex tourism, and the presence of military bases. Sexual exploitation is also found in business and work situations when consent is extracted by economic lure, coercion, and emotional blackmail. Sexual exploitation ramifies into different forms of political, economic, military and social oppression. The cry of women is the cry of the land, the cry of the little common folk, the cry of the minjung.

Jesus cried out for Jerusalem. His sorrow was so deep that Matthew had to use a "feminine metaphor" to describe what he actually felt: "How often would I have gathered your children together as a hen gathers her brood under her wings..." (Matt. 23:37). How much more would a mother lament over her dead son who died in the wars in Indochina? How can the mothers, wives, and lovers in Korea who are separated from their loved ones stop crying over the divided country?

Feminist theology in Asia is a story of suffering. What else can it be? Women suffer from the millennia-old prejudices and discriminations of the male-dominated Eastern cultures, from rampant socio-political exploitations, and from their structural vulnerability. These big burdens join hand-in-hand to rob a woman of her personhood, to render her a no-body.

Because suffering touches the innermost part of her being, she feels the pain of the suffering God: a God who cried out from the cross, who suffered under the oppressive Jewish tradition, a God who was put to death by the military and political forces, who was stripped naked, insulted and spat upon. Didn't the prophet Isaiah say: "He was despised and rejected by men, a man of sorrows and acquainted with grief, and as one from whom men hide their faces..." (Isa. 53:3)? God has taken the risk to become a human being, and experiences personally what it means to be a no-body.

It is the very person on the cross that suffers like us, was rendered a no-body, who illuminates our tragic human existence and speaks to countless women in Asia. We are not looking to Jesus as a mere example to follow, neither shall we try to idolize him. We see Jesus as the God who takes human form and suffers and weeps with us.

Dawning of the new

The story of women in Asia is a story of suffering. Zhang Zhi-xin was a revolutionary artist and composer, the mother of a son and a daughter. In the days of the Cultural Revolution, when the Gang of Four sent many innocent people to jail, she began to question the integrity and the policies of the government. She was labelled "anti-revolutionary" and was arrested in 1969. During the trial, this forty-year old mother turned the prosecution process into a debate on truth. Many times, the judge had to silence her because she was speaking the naked truth. Zhi-xin was finally executed in April 1975. Before the execution, the fascist officials ruthlessly cut her throat for fear that she would cry out over the suffering of the people before the public, even unto death.

In the farewell letter written to her husband in 1969, which was only released ten years later, Zhang Zhi-xin wrote:

> Married for fourteen years, we have one son and one daughter. I have not completed and cannot finish my duties. I hope you can try your best to bring up the new generation...
>
> I came to understand the revolution and determined to dedicate all of myself for the revolution!
>
> True revolutionary enterprise will be growing forever, stronger and stronger each day. Let us cheer for the bright and beautiful future. Cheer again for the victorious prospect. For the bright future, I wish to contribute my strength...[5]

Suk Wah (true name withheld) was formerly a student in Ehwa Women's University in Seoul. She organized study groups among the students and they discussed women's issues in Korea. She was caught and sentenced to two years' imprisonment because she led the group to read Engels's "The Origin of the Family, Private Property and the State" and other allegedly radical essays in order to find out the root causes of women's suffering. She was severely tortured. But far from losing hope, she began to read Letty Russell's "Human Liberation in a Feminist Perspective: a Theology" in her cell, and found much hope and encouragement.

In the struggle of Asian people, there are many nameless women like Zhi-xin and Suk Wah. Some of them may not have suffered so much, but all of them have a deep passion for their land. Traditionally, Asian women were quiet, subservient and gentle. Why do they break with tradition and dare to speak up? There must be an intuition, and a deep

---

[5] "Comrade Zhang Zhi-xin's Farewell Letter to Her Husband", *Chinese Women*, June 1979, p.11.

yearning inside, a passion that consumes the whole being so that one is no longer afraid.

This is a passion for justice. Women suffer and they know what suffering means. Many Zhi-xins and Suk Wahs must have heard the cry of the people and felt their pain. Whether they are educated or illiterate, middle-class or proletariat, conservative or radical does not matter. They are one with the people if their hearts are touched by their pain. It is this passion that makes them identify with the exploited, that motivates them and empowers them to rectify wrong, to fight for justice.

This is a passion for love. The gentle hands that swing the cradle, the soft voices that sing the lullaby, are filled with immense passion for love.

> The moon is so bright, shining on the front yard.
> Ha-tsai, be good and go to sleep on your bed.
> Tomorrow early morning, Mama has to transplant the rice-sprouts,
> Grandpa has to drive the cows to the mountains.
> Ha-tsai, grow fast and get taller,
> Row the boat, cast the net like those experienced.
> The moon is so bright, shining on the front yard.
> The New Year's eve, we eat betel-nuts,
> A good harvest and crops fill the store,
> The old and the young are gay and merry.
> Ha-tsai, quickly close your eyes and sleep till the morning breaks.[6]

This is the passion from the womb, as C.S. Song said. Women love their children and hope that everybody can live happily and peacefully. Women are more sensitive to others' feelings and they treasure relationships with others. In times of misfortune, a woman sacrifices herself to take care of the family. The love from the womb, the self-sacrifice of the mother, is the foundation for the passion of humankind.

This is a passion for hope. It is hope that lights up their way and gives them perseverance to go on. From the difficult situations of many women in Asia, it is not easy to speak of hope. Those women who stood by the cross and saw with their own eyes the death of Jesus would have felt that all their hope had gone. But Jesus first appeared to them after the resurrection. Out of grief and despair, once more, there comes hope. This new hope must have filled their whole being, for "they departed quickly from the tomb with fear and great joy" (Matt. 28:8).

Those women who saw the resurrection were entrusted with a task: to proclaim the good news to the people. Today, women all through Asia

---

[6] A very popular Cantonese lullaby. Author's translation.

who are gripped by this passion for justice, love and hope have a calling too, a calling that our friend in Sri Lanka, Kurinji Nathan, so beautifully described in a poem, "The New Woman":

The hands which gently tend the leaves
Will now help to banish darkness;
They'll work hard to put down evil,
And to raise up for all new life.

The hands which gently tend the leaves
Will help nourish all that is good;
They'll work hard to weed out poverty,
And bring in new culture and art.

The hands which gently tend the leaves
Will show new ways for humankind;
They'll work hard to build those structures
In which truth and right will be found.[7]

---

[7] See *For the Dawning of the New*, eds Jeffrey Abayasekera and D. Preman Niles, Singapore, CTC-CCA, 1981, p.42.

V. "Women that Make Asia Alive"

Marianne Katoppo

Asia is such a large continent of great diversity that it is difficult to claim any perspective as "Asian". We must remember that Asia has a very large population. Few of us pause to reflect that there are more women in India than the whole population of Western Europe. Also, Asia doesn't consist of only one race. All three races are represented. Furthermore, there are many language families in Asia, whereas Europe only knows the Indo-European and the Ural-Altaic. For example, Japan being a language family on its own, it is still very difficult for the Japanese to communicate with other Asians.

Therefore, it is a little presumptuous to claim any perspective as "Asian". It runs the risk of over-simplification and generalization, more so when we apply it to "women". Perhaps we could narrow it down to "women in the context of exploitation and oppression". Of course it is very important and timely to discuss this, for we live in an age when more Asian women are exploited than ever before in history.

At the moment 58 percent of the world's women live in Asia. The majority of them are oppressed and exploited. This is the reality. However, reality has many aspects. We must be able to distinguish between them, even as we distinguish myth from reality.

By "myth", I mean a blanket assumption or a sweeping statement that is too easily accepted, in order to legitimize a certain system or a certain structure.

The myth which is being widely promoted at the moment (consider airline advertisements and tourist brochures) is that "the Asian woman is gentle, placid, servile, docile", and so on (e.g. "Thai women's pleasure is to serve", "Singapore girl, you take care of me as only you know how", etc.). This projects a certain image of Asian women, which might please some men, but is certainly not representative of Asian women. We know how images can be really misleading, and trap persons into stereotypes.

When we talk about "Asian women", what do we really talk about? Japanese women are Asians, so are Filipinas, or Sri Lankans, or Lebanese. Geographically speaking, they all belong to the continent of Asia.

In Japan itself, one can distinguish between the aristocratic ladies of the *kazoku* (imperial household), the wives of salaried men, and the *burakumin*. In the Philippines, there are the complacent rich, with fat bank accounts in Switzerland, and then there are the women who have to leave their families in order to be able to earn food for them, doing all the things she cannot do for them for *other* people, in another country, i.e. by becoming domestic servants in Spain or Saudi Arabia.

In Sri Lanka, we are aware of the communal conflicts, and may fall into easy stereotypes. However, do we remember the Sinhalese nun, who was killed for sheltering Tamils, and do we know about the rich Tamil lady, with real estate in India and bank accounts in the United States?

At the very same time that the majority of Asian women are oppressed, some of the world's richest, most powerful, and also most materialistic women may be found right here in Asia.

Consider the late prime minister of India, Indira Gandhi. She wielded great power over millions of people. Then, in the Philippines, the wife of the previous president, Imelda Marcos, is a very pious woman who likes to pray the rosary. Her rosary consists wholly of diamonds, and one of her ambitions was to build a cathedral. In Thailand, there is Queen Sirikit, whom the mass media portray as a very beautiful and fashion-conscious woman. Beautiful she certainly is, and also very powerful. Last year, an outstanding Thai writer, Sulak Sivaraksa, was arrested and imprisoned on charges of *lèse majesté*, for "insulting the person of the queen".

Two hundred years ago, Mary Wollstonecraft said: "Birth, riches, and every extrinsic advantage which the human being has, and which does not need any more mental exertion, will turn that human being into a monster." (Of course Wollstonecraft used "man" instead of "human being".)

It is sad to see how true this often is in the Asian situation. To show you how impossible it is to generalize, I would like to mention here another Thai woman, who in my opinion is *the ideal Asian woman*. Interestingly enough, she is no other than the daughter of Queen Sirikit, Princess Maha Chakri Sirindhorn. Being the third child of the king and queen of Thailand, she didn't really qualify for the throne. However, on account of her strength of character and her personality, the constitution was changed a few years ago to make her crown princess (this is what Maha Chakri means), even though her elder brother, the crown prince, is still alive. A deeply religious person, she really wanted to be a Buddhist nun, but was persuaded it might be better to become queen instead. She is highly educated and has a strong sense of dedication and commitment. She does not abuse the power which is hers by birth. Wherever one goes in Thailand, even in the smallest villages in remote areas, one will find the portraits of the king... and the crown princess, *not* of the queen.

It is remarkable that this could happen in Asia, i.e. that the personality of a woman can bring about a change in constitution. Perhaps it shows us that the concept of leadership in Asia is not so gender-conscious as in Western Europe. In Sweden, the constitution was changed recently to make little Princess Victoria crown princess, but this was on account of primogeniture taking precedence over the Salian law, and had nothing to do with the personality of the princess.

The concept of women in high positions therefore is not something which is alien to Asia or borrowed from other cultures. In the Malay language, the word for woman is *perempuan*, from the root *empu*. This *empu* has many meanings. One of its primary meanings is "mother", e.g. *empu jari*, "mother (of) the fingers" — i.e. "the thumb", for you cannot really do anything without the thumb. *Empu* also means "sovereign", "a superior person": "superior" in the sense that this person is able to liberate, nurture, give life. (*Empu Mada*, "the Lord of Mada", was the most famous prime minister of the Hindu kingdom of Majapahit, and *Empu Sindok*, "Master Sindok", was the mystic teacher who through supernatural means separated the two kingdoms of Demak and Kediri.)

The other word used for "woman" in Malay is *wanita*, which is derived from Sanskrit, meaning "she whom all the world praises".

Language is the beginning of expression, and we should bear these expressions in mind. We cannot just use a kind of band-aid approach when we see how much oppression, misery and poverty there is, but we have to uncover the root causes of all the pain, suffering and injustice which we see all around us. We might attribute these to the political and economic structures. However, these structures are created by human beings, and it is rather unrealistic to think in certain categories only, like: "man-woman", "first world-third world", "rich-poor", "powerful-powerless", "oppressor-oppressed". In the majority of cases we could truthfully claim that "men oppress women", yet in a context like Asia there are also many men who suffer or live in conditions no better than women's.

Some women are also oppressors.

What we have to look for is the inner attitude which produces this kind of structure and this kind of system. In Asia, we might see that technology has become the modern idol; it is supposed to liberate us from poverty, to give us food, health, and a superior quality of life, and in many ways we sacrifice our people to this idol, forgetting that it is *false*, as all idols are.

We said that many women are suffering and oppressed. For example, in the electronic chips industry. The largest companies in electronics are IBM (US$26 billion turnover), General Electric (US$25 billion), ITT (US$18 billion), Philips, Siemens, Hitachi and Matsushita. So there are two Japanese among these giant electronic companies.

It is interesting to note in this context what one day's wages can buy for a female factory worker. In the Philippines, it would buy her 24 eggs. In Japan, 240 — ten times more. In Korea, 4 kilogrammes of rice; in Taiwan, almost 11 kg of rice. In Sri Lanka, one-fifth of a T-shirt. In Malaysia, one-fifth of a pair of jeans. In Thailand, half a pair of jeans. And in Hong Kong, one pair of jeans and four-fifths of a shirt.

These are the variables right within Asia. What, then, we may ask, is so terrible about the electronics industry? Electronic chips, for one, have caused many young female factory workers to lose their eyesight, because they have to peer down microscopes the better part of the day. The general practice is to dismiss them after three or four years, when they have become practically blind. A Unicef report has mentioned how child workers in Hong Kong often have become mutilated, because their small fingers are not fast enough and get crushed in the machines.

Recently, an American company in Indonesia refused its (women) workers the right to organize, so they went to the minister for human resources, who stated that it was their constitutional right to organize and to form a union. The American director, when interviewed by a leading newspaper, said in a tone of great surprise that he hadn't known that in Indonesia workers were allowed to organize.

It was a very silly argument to use: "I didn't know." A basic thing one does before setting up an enterprise in another country is to find out about the climate; in this case not just the temperature and level of humidity, but also the *critical* climate, which includes reading up on the labour laws.

This incident was a perfect illustration of some of the attitudes first world companies adopt towards the third world.

A very sharp increase in the migration of women is also one of the burning issues in Asia today. Whether they leave their homes to seek employment in factories in the big cities, or — as is becoming more and more common — as domestic servants in another country, the migration of women in Asia has reached terrifying proportions. At the moment it is estimated that over one million Filipinas, many of them with a college degree, are working abroad. It is appalling to think of the effect this will have on the social fabric.

In Osaka alone, every day 30 Filipinas are supposed to land. Recently, there was a case reported in Japanese papers of a man who had *bought* fourteen women at the price of 2 million yen. In Europe, the Piazza San Silvestro in Rome is crowded on Sundays with Filipinas who work there as domestic servants. A Filipina landing at Fiumicino airport nowadays is subjected to an interview with the police inspector before she is cleared for entry. In the eyes of many European authorities — and the person in the street — an Asian woman is a potential prostitute until proved otherwise.

We really have cause for concern. Firstly, as mentioned above, what does this kind of migration do to the fabric of life, to the society as such, because these women are all in the prime of life, and they should really be contributing to their societies, rather than going abroad to be slaves in another society.

Secondly, the image of Asian women is projected as that of the prostitute. German travel agents boast of the fact that "in the Philippines you can still make a woman happy with a handful of grapes, while at home in Germany she would be yours only for a fur coat". How insidious this image-building is came home to me forcefully when a European woman, educated, ecumenical, and all that, confessed to me that her first reaction when she saw a mixed couple, i.e. an Asian woman with a Western man, was to think: "Prostitute!"

In this kind of setting, how does one theologize? No high-falutin cerebral theology will do but an encounter with God at the gut-level. God who weeps with the mothers who have to abandon their homes to eke out a living in a foreign land. God who bears the insults heaped on woman, her image, because of her sex. God comforting all the non-persons (non-person because they are not rich, not male, not white) and assuring them that they are her beloved children. This is the theology we strive for, leading out Asia's oppressed daughters into the freedom of being.

VI. God in Man's Image

Louise Kumandjek Tappa

A question of power

It is clear that patriarchy did not start with Christianity. Jurgen Moltmann points out: "Patriarchy is a very ancient and widespread system of male domination. Christianity proved incapable of successfully opposing this system. Indeed, quite early on Christianity was already taken over by men and made to serve patriarchy."

I would like to suggest that Genesis 3:16, the classic text which has been used over the centuries to sanctify male domination, indicates that patriarchy is the oldest form of human domination. After the Fall, God says to the woman: "I will greatly multiply your pain in childbearing; in pain you shall bring forth children, yet your desire shall be for your husband, and he shall rule over you." This should be read as the description of a situation arising out of the order of sin. It is not God's prescription.

That Christianity has been captured by the patriarchal system is further attested by the fact that God is conceived in patriarchal vestments, God is presented in masculine terms and God's functions are reduced to male power roles. He reigns, he judges, he governs. He is almighty, fiercely jealous and possessive. He has none of the so-called female traits such as gentleness, tenderness, sensitivity, etc. Christianity has turned God into a prison warden. God is not different from the "macho"; usually absent from his home, yet served and feared; irascible and vindictive when he thinks he has been wronged. How can this picture reflect the God who "so loved the world that he gave his only son" and for whom the only commandment is love?

Patriarchy has created God in man's image. The ultimate idolatry! A most blatant manifestation of this idolatry is that women have been denied ordination on the simple basis of physiological nature.

Christianity teaches that the Holy Spirit is the active presence of God in and among us. This presence takes various forms and manifests itself freely. The Holy Spirit, we are told, moves when and where she wants. By excluding women from the ordained ministry, Christianity is clearly limiting God's action to the male sphere. God's word, it would seem, becomes God's word only when spoken by a he-man!

The Christian church thus functions as a male clan and uses God as its official seal.

It is obvious that the attributes of such a God can be defined only in terms that will legitimize and consolidate the "clan". As long as this God of Christianity is characterized in this way, there is no doubt that the concepts of justice and liberation cannot be fully integrated in our work and obviously our commitment to these issues will be weak. The distinction between a prophet and a minister of an organized religion has been more than adequately described by a character in Morris West's *The Clowns of God*.

> The minister of an organized religion was called and ordained to expound, under authority, a doctrine fixed and agreed long since. If he exceeded his commission he could be silenced or excommunicated by the same authority that called him. The prophet was another kind of creature altogether. He claimed a direct communication with the Almighty. Therefore, his commission could not be withdrawn by any human agent. He could challenge the most sacred past with the classic phrase, used by Jesus himself: it is written thus... but I tell you thus and thus.
>
> So the prophet was always the alien, the herald of change, the challenge of existing order.

Jesus died as a result of a clash between his God and the god of Pharisaic Judaism. Judaism had encaged God in its laws and tradition and its ministers could not accept a concept of God that went beyond their own limits. Says Jesus to the Pharisees: "For the sake of your tradition, you have made void the word of God" (Matt. 15:6). Jesus' crucifixion marked the temporal triumph of the patriarchal god of Judaism. His resurrection, however, proved that his God is the true God. His followers would therefore be expected to be committed to his God. But alas, Christianity has fallen back to the patriarchal god of Judaism with even greater zeal. The god of the institutionalized church now yields more power because the "clan" has become more powerful. The god of the clan will sanctify anything including militarism, war, sexism, apartheid, as long as it serves the interests of the clan. The god of the male clan will not have the interest of women at heart unless it benefits the males in some way.

It is my contention that the exclusion of women from effective participation in most aspects of church life is not so much based on biology. Sex only offers a ready-made excuse. The real issue is power.

Church structures are power-oriented. This is manifested in what is known as clericalism. The concept of the church leaves room for only one "minister" who is everything and does everything. Therefore there is no room for general participation. Church leaders and ministers too often substitute power and privilege for responsibility and service. They will not allow lay people to take an active part in the life of the church. A prominent church leader once was heard to say, as a lay training centre was being built, that lay training is a danger to pastorship. Thus, gifted laypeople (of both sexes) are regarded as rivals by church leaders and ministers. A passive congregation makes a powerful minister.

The issue raised by the women's liberation movement as it fights for equality and justice for women takes us to the heart of theology because they question our understanding of God. If God has from the beginning established a context of injustice by creating one social category that serves another, then that is unacceptable to people who believe in the true worth of all humankind.

Less than liberation

Our theology will not be credible if it opposes one system of oppression while championing another.

Catharina Halkes challenges us when she affirms that "in contrast to many other forms of theology of liberation, feminist theology is not to be pinned down in any particular locality. It cannot be defined in terms of national, tribal, racial or class boundaries." Women represent the other part of humanity without which there would be no humanity. They are oppressors and oppressed; they are rich and they are poor; they are yellow, black and white; women live in rural and urban areas, yet all of them experience male domination. In Rosemary Ruether's words, "sociologically, women are a caste within every class and race. As women, they share a common condition of dependence, secondary existence, domestic labour, sexual exploitation, and the projection of their role in procreation into a total definition of their existence. But this common condition is expressed in profoundly different forms as women are divided against each other by class and race." It is our contention, therefore, that, although feminist theology can also be enslaved by femaleness, the concept of liberation will begin to be fully understood only when it is also reflected upon in terms similar to what women have put forward. It is only then that theology will begin to be true to the word of God.

Black theology would not be addressing the issue of liberation fully if it only liberated itself from whiteness while it remained a slave of maleness. Liberation theology which has not had the wisdom to challenge the institutional elderly male dominations does not lead to liberation. A related illustration is the fact that in many instances women have actively taken part in the liberation struggles of their nations, and yet, when this "liberation" is achieved, men take up almost all the leadership positions.

Whatever way men have used the Bible to justify their lust for power, we know that the central message of the gospel is that of liberation. Liberation, not from creation, but from all forms of oppression that prevent human beings from being truly human. When Jesus says he came to "preach good news to the poor..., to proclaim release to the captives and recovery of sight to the blind, to set at liberty those who are oppressed, to proclaim the acceptable year of the Lord" (Luke 4:18-19), there is no doubt that he also meant the liberation of women from the bondage of patriarchy. Furthermore, liberating women from the bondage of patriarchy also means liberating men from the same bondage, for as Moltmann has pointed out, "oppression obviously has two sides: on the one side, there is the tyrant, on the other, the slave; here the dominating man and there the serving woman. Oppression destroys humanity on both sides: the oppressed person is robbed of humanity and the oppressor becomes an inhuman monster. But there is a difference: one of them suffers in consequence, whereas the other appears to feel fine. On both sides, however, liberation from oppression is needed." It is therefore not simply an issue of "women's liberation", but of enhanced humanization for all. God is not a God of oppression or domination and God's creation is not meant to live according to these principles. *Let God be God.*

Our theological task

Theology and the church should learn from the African concept of *Muntu*. Muntu is not simply a word that means person. It is a concept which includes both the physical and the spiritual person in community. A Muntu is not possible without Bantu: the spiritual in Muntu exists only in relation to Bantu. It is a community event which is not complete in personal ecstasy. If the spiritual is social, then it is also political. A Muntu approach to our work is thus called for.

The theology we need and the church (the people of God) that God calls forth are community-integrating. They should aim at helping each individual person (male and female, and regardless of age) to become truly human.

In other words, they should aim at promoting wholeness within the individual personality and the Christian community. This wholeness is made real in a given community when the members become aware of the fact that God gave "some to be apostles, some prophets, some evangelists, some pastors and teachers, for the equipment of the saints, for the work of ministry, for building up the body of Christ, until we all attain to the unity of the faith and of the knowledge of the Son of God, to mature manhood, to the measure of the stature of fullness of Christ" (Eph 6:11-13).

Wholeness for the individual and the community is therefore described in terms of self-fulfilment and awareness of one's responsibility in one's own context.

As Mollenkott rightly points out: "Christ's human nature was referred to by New Testament authors not as *aner*, male, but as *anthropes*, human. The implication of course, is that Christ became a person, rather than first and foremost a male. He came into the world, not only as the saviour of the world, but to provide the image of spiritual perfection of full physical and mental health, of the human ideal." In other words, Christ provides the ideal of wholeness for both male and female, possessing "wisdom and stature, and in favour with God and man" (Luke 2:52). He was physically and mentally healthy, and in perfect harmony with God and people. His saving activities aimed at giving humanity access to his wholeness.

He deliberately set himself against the powers that prevent people from attaining to wholeness: religious and cultural, economic and political.

Luke 11:27-28 is an essential text for our understanding of the liberation that Jesus brings to woman. Jesus' concern for full female personhood arises when a woman shouts his praises. "Blessed is the womb that bore you, and the breasts that you sucked." By these words, says Mollenkott, "Mary is reduced to one womb and two breasts". And indeed, "it is understandable that a first-century woman should think of herself and other women only as wives". Why seek a career since you have to respond to the noble vocation of motherhood? For Jesus blessedness transcends male or female biology. He says: "Blessed rather are those who hear the word of God and keep it."

Jesus does not deny that his mother is blessed. He says she is blessed because she responded positively to the word of God, not simply because she became a mother, even his mother. This statement implies that, for males as well as females, biology is not destiny. Our spiritual commitment is our destiny. Consequently, blessedness is open to all single women, childless women, mothers; it is open to men and children as well as women. It is open to all of us whether male or female, healthy or crippled.

The only thing that really matters is our willingness or unwillingness to adhere to the plan of God for humanity. The church is the people of God, called to witness and to embody the values and norms of the kingdom of God initiated by Jesus Christ. As new creatures in Christ, Christians are called to resist the worldly principles of dominance and submission which are the results of sin. We must therefore work for a participatory community so that men and women of all ages become acceptable in all areas of Christian ministry and church governance. We must move from "brotherhood" to a fellowship of brothers and sisters, making real the teaching of the gospel that male and female are made in the image of God and are both God's stewards on earth.

To do this, the church must first and foremost recognize the sinfulness of patriarchy, a social system oppressive and dehumanizing for both men and women, and consequently rid itself of those structures that reflect patriarchal ideals. It must endeavour to educate the people towards wholeness as the ultimate goal for humanity, empowering them to attain this goal. When Peter and John encountered the lame man at the gate of the temple, they did not resort to giving him alms at which the Jews were experts; they gave him what he needed to become whole — the use of his legs (Acts 3:1-8). The challenge to the church is to express the love of God by eradicating all the structures and powers that prevent people from attaining wholeness and by creating circumstances and opportunities for all to become truly human.

Contributors

Elizabeth Amoah, a Ghanaian Methodist, is lecturer in the Department for the Study of Religions at the University of Ghana, Legon.

Elsa Tamez from Mexico is a Methodist and a staff member of the Latin American Biblical Seminary, Costa Rica.

Lee Oo Chung, a Korean, is a member of the Presbyterian Church and president of the Korean Women Theologians Association.

Julia Esquivel, living in exile, is a Guatemalan poetess, educator, activist and Christian spokesperson for the cause of justice in her country and in Central America, and a founder of the Committee for Justice and Peace in Guatemala.

Marie Assaad, of the Egyptian Coptic Orthodox Church, is moderator of the WCC's Unit III "Education and Renewal".

Grace Eneme, a Presbyterian from Cameroun, works on women's programmes for FEMEC (Federation of Protestant Churches and Missions in Cameroun) member churches, and is a member of the WCC Central Committee.

Maria Teresa Porcile, a Roman Catholic from Uruguay, is a theologian working on a doctorate at the University of Fribourg, Switzerland.

Priscilla Padolina, of the United Methodist Church in the Philippines, is programme secretary on women and rural development in the WCC's Sub-unit on Women in Church and Society.

Mercy Oduyoye, Ghanaian by birth and Nigerian by marriage, is a Methodist. She is senior lecturer in the Department of Religious Studies of the University of Ibadan, Nigeria.

Elizabeth Dominguez, a Filipino, is professor of Old Testament at Union Theological Seminary in Manila, Philippines.

Aruna Gnanadason, a member of the Church of South India, is executive secretary of the All India Council of Christian Women, and vice-moderator of the WCC's Sub-unit on Women in Church and Society.

Mahat Farah El-Khoury, a Syrian of the Greek Orthodox Church, is part-time staff member of the Middle East Council of Churches and a writer on peace issues and women's concerns.

Bette Ekeya, a Kenyan Roman Catholic, is on the staff of the Department of Religious Studies, University of Nairobi, Kenya.

Virginia Fabella, a Roman Catholic from the Philippines, teaches religious education and is executive secretary of the Ecumenical Association of Third World Theologians.

Kwok Pui Lan, an Anglican from Hong Kong, is lecturer at the Chung Chi College, Division of Theology, Hong Kong.

Marianne Katoppo, a Presbyterian from Indonesia, is a theologian and journalist and a writer on women's issues.

Louise Tappa, from Cameroon, is a Baptist and a staff member of the All Africa Conference of Churches in Nairobi.